Singing to the World
MARIAN ANDERSON

Britannica Bookshelf—Great Lives

Singing to the World

MARIAN ANDERSON

by Janet Stevenson

26, 830

Published by
ENCYCLOPAEDIA BRITANNICA PRESS, INC., *Chicago*

The editors would like to thank the Johnson Publishing Company, particularly Doris Saunders, head of the book division, for their cooperation in opening their picture files for our use.

Permission to quote from Mrs. Franklin Delano Roosevelt's column, "My Day," copyright, 1939, has been granted by United Feature Syndicate, Inc.

TABLE OF CONTENTS

Chapter 1

A Time to Fight?

The special delivery was postmarked Washington, D.C., January 19, 1939.

It was delivered early, before there was any one in the office, dropped through the slot under the sign on the door that said:

HUROK ATTRACTIONS

The telephone operator picked the letter up when she came to work. There were already three lights flashing on her switchboard; so she dropped the letter on the desk of the boss's assistant and hurried to answer the calls.

The first was from Paris, where it was already afternoon. The next was from San Francisco, where it was not yet daylight. The third was from Carnegie Hall, just a few blocks away across the center of New York City. After that things settled down into the ordinary routine of a day in the office of a concert manager.

[7]

It is a very complicated business, concert managing. A dozen different sorts of experts are needed. There must be lawyers to draw up contracts between the manager and the artists whose affairs he handles. There must be press agents to write articles for newspapers and magazines, to see that pictures are taken and distributed, and to work out details of advertisements, posters, and programs. There are people who only handle "bookings"—arrangements for concerts with managers in other cities—planning a tour so the performer will travel more or less in a straight line, without zigzagging or doubling back too often.

When the tour is all planned and the bookings made, an expert on transportation takes over, buys railroad or airline tickets—or charters a bus or hires a car—making sure that the performer or a whole troupe of performers with scenery and costumes, in some cases, can get wherever they are going in time for their next appearance. Someone else is the hotel expert, responsible for seeing to it that there is a reservation in each of the 10 or 20 or 30 cities on the schedule, for a temperamental South American pianist who wants to be sure of quiet, or for a chorus of former Cossacks who want to be free to make plenty of noise.

In the case of a manager who handles many foreign artists, there must also be interpreters, people who can translate in and out of English for people who speak only Swedish, or Hungarian, or one of the languages of India or Africa.

The staff of Hurok Attractions was a miniature army under the command of a short, stout, Russian-born general, who carried a gold-headed cane instead of a sword, and wore a black fedora hat instead of a campaign cap. His second-in-command was a cheerful, down-to-earth American woman named Mae Frohman. It was she who opened the special delivery from Washington that morning.

"Oh, but that makes me angry," she said as she read it.

"What does?" asked the man at the desk next to hers.

Mae handed him the letter, which was addressed to S. Hurok, and which read as follows:

I am writing to you of our difficulty in securing an auditorium for Miss Marian Anderson who is to sing for us on April 9th. We have made application to Constitution Hall, which is in our judgement the only hall in Washington suitable for an appearance by Miss Anderson.

We are informed by Fred E. Hand, manager of the Hall, that a clause in the rental contract prohibits the presentation of Negro artists. The Hall, as you know, is owned and operated by the Daughters of the American Revolution.

If there is anything you can do to persuade those in authority to change the policy so that Miss Anderson's concert can take place there, we shall appreciate it greatly.

Charles Cohen, Chairman,
Howard University Concert Series.

"Marian Anderson has the greatest singing voice in America, and they can't find a hall for her!" Mae said, and took the letter back.

She marched into Sol Hurok's private office without bothering to knock on the door.

"What are we going to do about this?" she asked indignantly and slapped it down on his desk, as if it were somehow all his fault.

Hurok read the letter through. When he looked up at last, there was no sign of surprise or anger on his face. It was the face of a showman who knew when to express and when to conceal his feelings, the face of a man who could respond to art and beauty when he let himself, but who could also fight in the business arena with the cold skill of a gladiator.

"What do they expect me to do?" he asked.

"You can at least write to the manager," Mae said.

"And say what? 'Please change your stupid policy so that one of America's greatest artists can be heard in your city?' The manager will wire back and say, 'Mind your own business and I'll mind mine.' "

"How do you know unless you try?" Mae demanded.

"Because, in the first place, he does not make this policy. It is made by the owners. They hire him to carry it out."

"Then wire the owners, the Daughters of the American Revolution."

"Who are these Daughters?" Hurok asked. "What do you know about them?"

"They're ladies who can trace their ancestry back to someone who fought in the war for American independence," Mae said. "I wonder if anyone ever told them that there were Negroes who fought in that war. For all we know Marian Anderson may be descended from one of them. That would make her eligible to join the D.A.R.!"

"Why don't you write the letter?" Hurok asked with a smile. "I'll sign anything that isn't libel."

Back at her desk, Mae worked on a letter of polite but urgent protest. She showed it to Gerald Goode, the press agent.

"You're the writer around here," she said. "Tell me if this is too strong."

"It's not strong enough for the way I feel," Goode said when he had read it. "But I doubt if anybody's letter is going to change a policy like that."

Mae looked so discouraged that he said, "I'll tell you what I'll do. I have to make the rounds of the newspapers this afternoon. Let me ask around and see how other people feel. Especially newspaper people who can put their feelings in linotype. If enough of them start steaming, maybe we can get up some real pressure."

"Thank you, Gerry," Mae said fervently.

"Don't thank me yet."

When Goode came into the office the next day, what he had to report was so exciting that a strategy conference was called in Hurok's office.

"I talked to men on half a dozen New York papers and two national news services," Goode said. "Every single one of them felt the way we do: that this is a crying shame."

"Crying does no good," said Hurok. "Will they write about it?"

"Yes. If we can prove that the turndown was because Marian Anderson is a Negro."

"What is there to prove?" asked Mae. "The manager told the man from Howard that was the reason."

"Take a look at this, " Goode said. He brought out of his pocket a clipping from the Washington *Herald*. "Evidently someone at Howard wrote an open letter to the newspapers before Mr. Cohen wrote us."

The clipping was from the editorial column of the *Herald*, dated January 15, 1939:

It stands almost in the shadow of the Lincoln Memorial, but the Great Emancipator's sentiments about 'race, creed or previous condition of servitude' are not shared by the Daughters, for every contract for the use of these halls contains a clause banning any member of the Negro race. . . . Prejudice rules to make the Capital of the Nation ridiculous in the eyes of all cultured people and to comfort Fuehrer Hitler and the members of our Nazibund.

"That's fine," said Mae enthusiastically. "If a few more papers run editorials like that, maybe things will begin to happen."

"Wait till you hear what's already happened," Goode warned her. "The day after the editorial appeared, the paper got a sheaf of angry letters. Members of the D.A.R. writing in to say that their organization had been slandered! One of the ladies had called Constitution Hall and asked about the Marian Anderson matter. She was told that the Hall had been refused because it was already rented to somebody else."

"I don't believe it!" Mae exclaimed.

"You don't believe that's what they told the lady? Or you don't believe they told her the truth?" asked Hurok, and handed her a telegram he had just received, the answer to her protest letter.

BEG TO ADVISE YOU THAT CONSTITUTION HALL IS NOT AVAILABLE ON APRIL 9TH BECAUSE OF PRIOR COMMITMENTS.
FRED E. HAND

"I just don't understand," Mae said. "If they told Mr. Cohen it was a policy . . . "

"Somebody has decided he doesn't want any trouble," said Gerry Goode.

"Somebody—or *somebodies* want to have things their own way and still not have any trouble," said Mae.

"And you want to make trouble," said Hurok. "But Marian won't. She won't push herself in any place she is not welcome. You know that."

"I don't know that it's for her to decide this time," Mae said. "It seems to me there's something more important involved than her personal feelings or even what's good for her career. She's a symbol of something. . . . "

"Maybe she's a symbol, but she's not a fighter," said Hurok bluntly. "If you pick up the phone and call her right now, you know what she'll tell you? Forget it! Cancel the Howard University date!"

"I'm not asking her to fight," Mae said stubbornly. "I'm saying we ought to fight for her. Here she is, trying to use her voice as it was meant to be used, to give people pleasure and—yes, inspiration! And having to put up with insults and slights and sometimes real hardships!"

[*13*]

Sol Hurok and Marian Anderson, 1939

"Look, Mae, we agree. We know—"

"You know part, but not all of it!" Mae was not going to be interrupted this time. "If you'd travelled with Marian as I have on tour in the South, you'd know a lot more.

"Take for instance all that luggage she carries with her —the extra things like the portable typewriter and the sewing machine and the ironing board. I've heard you kid her about it, tell her that she could hire a maid and a secretary for what she has to pay in excess baggage charges. Maybe you think Marian writes her own business letters and presses her own concert dresses and even makes curtains on tour to save money!

"But she does it to save herself!

"She works to keep from getting angry or bitter or lonely. She works at her music or anything else she can

[14]

find to work at, to forget the hurts. To rise above them! Quietly, proudly—because she's the proudest person I know!

"And that's what I mean about her being a symbol of something. I don't know exactly how to say it, but it has something to do with that spirit in her people that keeps them proud, and still able to give what's theirs to give in spite of people who reject it because they like pink skin better than brown!"

No one—not even Mae herself—had expected to hear such an emotional speech from her. They were all hard-boiled business people, used to dealing with the world the way it is, leaving it for preachers and politicians to worry about changing it.

"You know someone who feels the way you do, Mae?" Goode said after a moment of embarrassed silence. "Walter White of the National Association for the Advancement of Colored People. I talked to him yesterday."

"Now there's a real spark plug!" said Hurok. "And this is right up his alley! Why doesn't he take it on?"

"He wants to. In fact, he's already sent out wires to a lot of prominent people asking them to protest to the D.A.R. But he doesn't believe that's going to do the trick. Not in time for this particular concert. He wants the people at Howard to start looking for another place."

"There's no other place in Washington that's good enough," said Hurok. "I won't have Marian go back to singing in churches. I'd rather see her sing free in a park!"

"Personally I'm not ready to give up on Constitution Hall," Goode said. "I've been thinking a lot about those D.A.R. members who were so angry with the editor of the

Herald. If we could prove to them that what he wrote was true, they'd be angry with their own officers instead. And if there are enough members like that, their officers will have to change their policy."

"How are you going to prove it? Wait till April 9th and see if someone else has rented the hall? By that time somebody else probably will."

"I want to prove it right now," said Goode. "And I think I know how. But I'd have to ask a favor of someone. A big favor! One I don't want to ask unless we're sure we're going to put up a real fight."

"What favor? From whom?" asked Hurok, who didn't like asking favors from anyone.

Goode didn't answer directly. Instead he went on thinking aloud, sketching the outlines of the trap he wanted to spring.

"We need someone who represents a world-famous artist. We want him to inquire about dates when Constitution Hall can be rented—dates as near as possible to April 9. It must be someone not connected with this office so no suspicions are aroused.

"Now—if the inquiry is for a concert by an artist who's a big enough drawing card, Manager Fred Hand will give a list of open dates. Then we let the people at Howard University know what they are. They put in a request for one or all of them. They'll be refused, because that's the policy.

"And there's our proof!"

"But no manager will make an inquiry if he has no intention of renting the hall," said Hurok uneasily. "It's bad business practice. I wouldn't do it myself."

"I wouldn't ask anyone to do it unless I could tell him that you *would* do it yourself under these circumstances," Goode said, putting it up to him squarely.

There was quite a long silence.

"Who is it you're thinking about asking?"

"Marks Levine," answered Goode. "He's got Paderewski on tour this season. I doubt if any manager would turn down a request for him."

There was another silence. Hurok stirred in his big leather swivel chair and muttered under his breath.

"Like you say, it's not right to ask such a favor unless we're going to make a fight. This would only be the beginning."

"That's true. Only the beginning of a long, hard— maybe an ugly fight! But this is part of a much bigger fight that the whole country is facing," Goode said. "One that may turn into a war before it's over! If we can't win such a fight in America today, then what's going to happen when—"

"You don't have to lecture me about America!" Hurok snapped angrily. "Remember, please, I am an American by choice! I know what I have chosen! Better maybe than you!

"I also know Marian Anderson," he continued, "better even than Mae here. I know what she means in the countries of Europe. I have heard her sing in their capitals. I know how it sounds that she cannot sing in her own.

"But I know that she will not want to make bad publicity for her country. She will not want to blame any group—not even these Daughters of the American Revolution—for what may be the action of a few individuals. That's

[17]

how she will put it, if you put it up to her.

"As for me, I have never minded a fight yet. I'm not sure I would not be glad of such a good reason to start one. I'm sick of being ashamed of how many places we can't make a hotel reservation for Marian on tour, or how many trains won't sell first-class space for her.

"The question is can we fight for someone who doesn't want to be fought for? Can we finish such a fight if we start it?"

Gerry Goode and Mae Frohman looked at each other in amazement. It was certainly a day for speechmaking. Neither of them had ever heard Sol Hurok talk like that. They understood that the anger in his voice was not meant for them. He was fighting some battle inside himself.

They waited, without speaking, for him to announce the outcome.

Hurok was thinking back over the three years he had been Marian Anderson's manager . . . looking into the past for the answer to the question that might decide the future . . . remembering the first night he had heard her sing . . . the night that marked the turning point in her career, the beginning of her real rise to fame. . . .

Chapter 2

Discovery

I t was a lovely June evening in Paris, the first stop on his yearly tour in search of new attractions—singers and dancers, orchestras and choruses, puppeteers, and pianists, new-comers or established artists—to present in the United States during the coming season. The tour might take Hurok to almost any corner of the world before it was over, but it always began in Paris, with a few leisurely days to enjoy the city, to meet old friends and new ones, to rest before the real traveling began.

He and Mrs. Hurok were sipping their after-dinner coffee at an outdoor cafe table along the treelined boulevard of the Champs Elysées. The light of the nearest street lamp fell in a bright stripe across the name on a poster announcing a concert. The name kept nagging at Hurok's memory till at last he turned to his wife.

"Who is Marian Anderson?" he asked.

She thought a moment and then shook her head. "I don't think I've ever heard of her."

Hurok had. But where, he could not for the moment recall.

Soon they were joined by a group of acquaintances in the musical world, one of them a critic on a large Paris newspaper. Hurok repeated his question and instantly they were all talking at once.

"Marian Anderson? The finest contralto voice I have ever heard!" said the music critic.

"A well trained oriole, masquerading as a woman," said someone else, perhaps a poet.

"An American! You ought to know her better than we."

"She won all sorts of prizes in your country before she came over here."

Now Hurok remembered. People had told him about a young Negro singer who won an important national contest one summer while he was away. Whoever reported this had urged him to go to a recital she was giving in some church. Was it in Philadelphia? At any rate he was too busy at the time. He meant to catch up with her later, but somehow there was never another convenient opportunity, and eventually he forgot all about it.

"I can't believe you've never heard her! What an experience you have missed," the critic was saying.

"I won't miss it any longer," said Hurok and turned to his wife to ask, "You're not very tired, are you? How about dropping in for just a few songs?"

She laughed. "I know what that means. You'll stay to the last encore. Go on without me. I have to unpack."

"I doubt you'll be able to get a seat at this late hour," someone said. "Her last concert was nearly sold out. This one surely will be."

"If I can't sit, I'll stand," said Hurok.

A few minutes later, he had dropped his wife at their hotel and was hurrying up the steps of the Salle Gaveau, his travel weariness forgotten in the excitement that always filled him at the prospect of making a new discovery. It was this that made his work more than just business, something like the adventure of exploring.

The hall was sold out, but the manager was an old acquaintance of his, Fritz Horowitz whom he had known in Berlin. It was professional courtesy to accomodate a fellow manager in any case. A chair was placed for him in the rear of the box closest to the stage.

Hurok had just time to settle himself before the singer and her accompanist came out. A tall, handsome, dark-skinned young woman, with great dark eyes and shiny black hair, dressed in a golden gown that seemed to glow in the cool gray of the stage space. A tall, handsome, fair-skinned man in formal evening dress. Kosti Vehanen and Marian Anderson, what a contrasting pair! How had they come to be teamed together?

The murmuring audience quieted. The piano sounded softly. The singer closed her eyes and seemed to withdraw into herself.

From somewhere—it didn't seem to be her mouth—came a thread of song, a long, light, silvery trilling. Schubert's "Bird Song"! But that was written for a soprano voice! Someone at the cafe table had said, "She has four voices in one!" She certainly did have an extraordinary range, Hurok thought. The high register was good, very good. But what about the middle voice, the one that made her a contralto, if that was what she was?

The next selection was an aria from a French opera. Before it was over, he had forgotten about range and register. He was in the grip of a power he had seldom felt in a concert hall. It was as if the whole force of this woman's soul were focused into a beam of sound that was aimed at him, as if she were singing directly to him, trying to tell him something that could not be put into words, something of the deepest importance. . . .

Yet she was not even looking in his direction. She was not looking anywhere. Her eyes were still closed. Her face was lifted slightly as if she were receiving as well as sending inspiration into the air above her.

He could feel tears pressing against his eyelids, and he struggled against them. He was not here to give way to his emotions like an ordinary spectator. He was here to use his head, to make a cold, clear judgment, to decide whether this young woman's voice, musicianship, and personality added up to that mysterious total which makes what is called in show business "a top attraction." How could he figure the angles if he let himself go soft at the start like this?

The next song ended the struggle and brought on the tears. It was an ancient lullaby that he had never heard before, in a language he did not understand. But it haunted him as if he had heard it in his own cradle days. What she

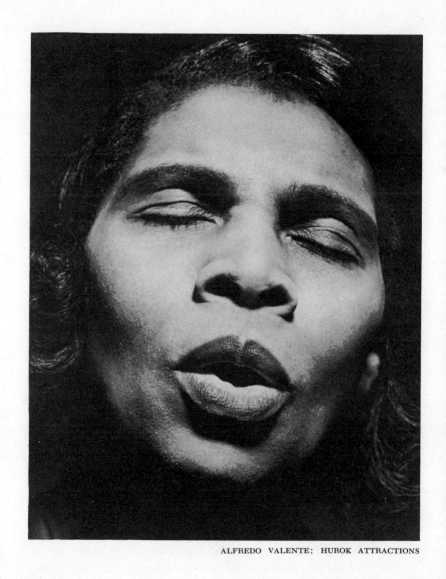

ALFREDO VALENTE: HUROK ATTRACTIONS

Vocalizing

sang after that he hardly knew, until the last number of the group brought him suddenly back to earth.

It was a wild, exuberant sailor's song, written by the pianist especially for the singer. The applause came crashing like a tidal wave as the last chord struck. The audience was on its feet, clapping and stamping and shouting, more like excited American teen-agers than sophisticated Parisians.

The composer stood at the keyboard and bowed and smiled, first to the audience, then to the singer, who bowed and smiled, bowed and smiled, cool and serene.

"Would you like to meet her?"

It was his friend, Horowitz, at his elbow.

Hurok nodded and followed him down the stairs to the stage door, through a narrow passageway to a door marked with a somewhat tarnished painted star.

Horowitz knocked. A velvety voice invited him to come in. They opened the door and entered the dressing room.

The woman to whom Hurok was presented was so shy that he could hardly believe it was the same one who had played so powerfully with an audience's emotions only a few minutes before. Her speaking voice was beautiful, but breathy, as if she were a little upset. (Marian confessed to him long afterwards that she was a little upset, and for good reason, but he did not understand it then.)

He knew it was bad manners to waste a singer's precious minutes of rest at intermission, so he asked if it would be convenient for her to meet him at another time.

"We shall be leaving Paris very soon," she said, hesitantly. "We have an engagement in Brussels next week."

"Let it be tomorrow morning. At 11, if that is not too early."

"Eleven will be fine. But where?"

"In Mr. Horowitz's office?"

"Very well," she said, still a little hesitantly. "We shall be there."

Hurok did not go back to the hotel. As Mrs. Hurok had predicted, he went back to his seat to listen again, to be sure he had heard right the first time, that the magic was really there in her voice.

The final group of songs was all the reassurance he needed. They were spirituals: some humorous, some tragic, songs he had heard many times before. He had heard them sung by such famous artists as the Negro tenor, Roland Hayes, by such great choruses as the Fisk Jubilee Singers, by untrained voices in Negro churches. But he had never heard them sung like this.

The beautiful dark face was a mask behind which the singer disappeared. The song that poured through lived its own life and spoke directly to the listener, spoke of love and of grief, of despair and exultation and deep religious peace, each in turn. In the silence when she was finished, he could hear people sob.

Long after the last bow had been taken, people were still clapping, not wildly, as they had for the earlier groups, but on and on, without letup. No one seemed to want to go home. They stood in the aisles, or drifted down toward the stage, still clapping and calling "Bravos" as if they couldn't bear to be separated from the woman who had worked such wonders in their hearts.

Promptly at 11 next morning, Hurok arrived at the office of Mr. Horowitz. Marian was already there. She had brought the other half of the team she referred to when she said "we." (Hurok was to learn that she almost always said "we," hardly ever "I.")

As was his custom in this sort of interview, Hurok took command from the start, directing his questions toward the most important facts from a business point of view:

How many concerts had she given the last season she sang in the United States? How long ago was that?

What fees had she received on the average? What was the highest? The lowest?

On what concert series had she appeared?

In what concert halls had she sung? In New York, in Philadelphia, in San Francisco, and so on.

As she answered his questions, sometimes stopping to think, sometimes not needing to, Hurok was getting answers to other unspoken questions that were just as important:

What sort of woman was this who hid herself behind the facade of quiet politeness?

How hard a worker? How persistent? How sensitive? How ambitious? How temperamental?

All these were qualities that would count in the battle he had in mind. For he could see now that it was going to be a battle if he decided to take on the management of her American career.

He had done a lot of thinking during the night. He had asked and answered the question of why such a magnificent voice had gone practically unnoticed in its homeland. It was very simple: because she was a Negro.

[26]

Americans were not accustomed to hearing Negro singers in concert except in what they considered Negro music: folk songs and spirituals. Marian Anderson was what is called an "art singer." She sang the classical and modern masters, from Bach and Handel to Sibelius and Debussy. For many Americans the color of her skin and the color of her music did not match.

Marian admitted to him frankly that she had come to Europe in the hope of winning critical approval that would help her break into top concert circles at home. It was a perfectly sound plan. It had worked for many another American performer, white as well as Negro, and it would again.

"I have had some success in Europe," Marian told him, "especially in the Scandinavian countries."

(Hurok had heard from Horowitz just how great that success was. He learned now that she had another virtue—modesty—something one did not often meet in a prima donna.)

"But it made almost no difference at home," she said. She didn't blame the management that had been handling her affairs, though Hurok considered that she had good reason to complain. But she had no feeling of obligation that would prevent her leaving if she could do better for herself with another manager.

That was all.

She had finished. It was his turn to speak.

"I think I might be able to do better for you," he said cautiously. "If you will come back to New York at the height of the season, and stay at least four months, I will guarantee you 15 concerts."

He named a fee. It was not much higher than the one she had told him was her average, and she had sung more than 15 concerts her last season at home.

It was not a flattering offer.

On the other hand, to guarantee 15 concerts meant to risk a great deal of money, for it was a promise to pay her fee and all expenses, no matter what came in at the box office. If she had good business sense, she would understand that this meant he believed he could make a great success with her. Otherwise, it would not be worth the risk. If she believed in him and in herself, she would accept the offer.

He watched her face while she thought about it. She was taking her time. Good! Hurok respected the person who took time to make decisions and made them to last.

"Very well," she said quietly. "I will come back in December." Then she turned to Vehanen. "What about you, Kosti?"

"You know I want nothing so much as a chance to visit America," Vehanen answered. "But will it make problems for you to have me as your accompanist?"

For the first time in the interview, Marian seemed uneasy. "There is one problem," she admitted. "Billy King was always my pianist in concerts at home. We haven't worked together for a long time, because I haven't been home for a long time. . . . I owe him a great deal. Of course, I owe you a great deal, too, Kosti. . . . But he was a good friend when I needed one. . . ."

It was obviously painful for her to make comparisons between the two. Hurok could sympathize, but he couldn't help.

[28]

"You must not worry about hurting anyone's feelings," Vehanen advised her. "It is not the people, but the music that matters. You must decide on professional grounds only."

It wasn't as simple as that, Hurok thought to himself, though a Finnish musician could hardly be expected to know why not.

He had no prejudice against people of a different color, nor did the audiences before whom he and Marian had appeared. But it would be different in America. Especially in the South. There would be some white people who disapproved of a white man serving as accompanist to a Negro woman. They would make sure their disapproval was publicized. Negro audiences might disapprove for the opposite reason. Many would resent what looked like turning her back on her own people and disloyalty to her old friend, Billy King.

The decision Marian was making now was crucial. The way she made it would be a clue to what could be expected from her in other crises.

She looked over at Hurok as if giving him a chance to speak if he wanted to, but he shook his head. It was up to her.

The silence was stretching out into an uncomfortable suspense.

"I'm afraid this is something I can't decide now," Marian said finally. "May I take a little time?"

Both men assured her that she could take as long as she liked, and the conference broke up.

Several weeks later, Hurok had a letter from Marian.

By this time she had had one of her greatest surprise triumphs, but there was nothing about that in the letter. She wrote only to tell him that she had finally decided the question of who was to be her pianist. It would not please everyone, and many people would jump to the conclusion that it was her new manager who was responsible. There would be no chance to explain that this was not true, nor that she had made the decision only after exploring every other possibility.

"My people are right to expect that if an opportunity is open, one of our own should not be bypassed," she wrote. "But a Negro must qualify on musical grounds if he is to find a place. On the other hand—and this is what makes it so hard for me—there is no incentive for a young musician to work hard and learn to be a first-class accompanist if he knows there will be no place open to him."

It was truly a vicious circle, and there was no perfect answer. But each decision had to be made on the facts of that case. Marian had tried to find a qualified accompanist among her own people. There were not many, and all she knew had turned out to be engaged.

"So I have asked Mr. Vehanen to continue with me, and he has been kind enough to agree."

It was all there in the letter, the whole woman: her seriousness, her loyalty, her tactfulness and courtesy, her deliberate way of working out a problem, and the finality of her decision once it was made.

Hurok believed it was the right decision, made on the right grounds. From here on most of the decisions would be up to him. He only hoped he could do as well.

Chapter 3

The Jinx

Back in New York, Hurok set about making the preparations for what he thought of as the launching of a new career.

It was harder in some ways because it was not really new. Marian had sung many years of concerts in the United States. She had even sung a debut concert in New York's Town Hall, but it was before she was ready and it was a dismal failure. After that she had some important successes, one of them in New York. But successes and failures were blurred in people's memories by the years she had stayed in Europe.

"When an artist doesn't make it after as many tries as she's had, it's like a jinx," one of his friends warned him. "You can't explain it, but you can't get around it."

"You'll be lucky if you break even on 15 concerts," another said.

"You won't be able to give her away!" was the cruelest of the comments.

"Wait and see," Hurok replied to them all.

He meant to do much better than break even. He had no intention of giving Marian's services away. He was gambling on nothing less than a smash hit!

He knew that success must come with her first New York concert, or it would probably not come at all. That concert must be at Town Hall, at the height of the winter season. The top critics must be there, and Marian must sing at her superb best. They must write the sort of reviews that could (and would) be quoted all over the country.

If that happened, the next 14 concerts would be a series of triumphs. if not . . .

But Hurok didn't let himself worry about "if not's." Let the doubters do that. He had plenty to keep him busy.

For he was sponsoring this first, all-important "Triumphal Return Engagement" himself. It was not part of any established concert series. The program would read:

"Sol Hurok Presents—"

He would pay for that program and for the hall and the advertising—everything. This was not customary for an artist who was not yet established. Such a person was usually glad to pay all or part of his expenses. But Hurok never operated that way.

For one thing, if he was going to gamble, he liked to gamble with his own money. For another, he thought asking an artist to pay expenses had a bad effect on morale.

There was just enough of the artist's temperament in his own makeup, so that he understood what an ordeal a debut concert was for a high-strung, sensitive musician. He knew how important it was to believe in one's self at such a time, and how much it helped to know that others believed. He knew no better way to show his confidence than by laying out in advance the hard cash, from the down payment on the rental of Town Hall to the last line of advertising in the New York *Times*. It was his bet, placed —as they say at the race track—on the nose.

There were many details to be arranged, most of them having to do with putting the audience—especially the critics—in the best possible frame of mind. It was important, for instance, that Americans should know what had been said about Marian Anderson abroad. He had copies of reviews from Danish and Swedish and French newspapers translated into English and sent in advance to newspaper and magazine music departments. It was important to have it known that Maestro Arturo Toscanini, conductor of the New York Philharmonic Orchestra, had heard her sing this past summer and had praised her most extravagantly.

On the other hand, one could go too far with this sort of publicity. People don't like to be told what to think, especially if they are paid to have their own opinions, as critics are. Too much quoting from Europeans might put American critics in a mood to find fault. It was a delicate problem in diplomacy.

And so on down to the question of how big the type on the posters should be. No pains were spared to foresee and provide for everything, to take every possible advantage, to avoid every possible pitfall.

But in the end it always seemed to come down to a matter of luck.

For there is always something unforeseeable that makes the difference between success and failure. Perhaps that's why people in show business so often talk in the same terms as gamblers—of jinxes and hunches, and runs of luck, good or bad.

In this case, the first piece of luck was the sort that could lose the stakes before the wheel was spun.

When he met the boat that was bringing Marian and Vehanen from Europe, Hurok knew that something was wrong. Marian looked well. She was becomingly dressed and her manner was serene, as always. But there was something in her face . . . something in the way she carried herself.

He took Vehanen aside and questioned him.

"What's wrong with Marian? Is she unhappy? Is she in love? Is she sick?"

At first Vehanen tried to squirm out from under the questions, but finally he gave in.

"She has asked me not to speak of it to anyone," he said apologetically. "But after all, one's manager is not anyone. What is wrong is that there was an accident on shipboard. Marian hurt her foot."

Hurok watched her walking across the room where all luggage was inspected by customs officers. Her foot was not bandaged and she was not exactly limping, but he could see now that she was making a great effort not to show that she was in pain.

"What happened? How bad is it?"

Vehanen was not sure how bad it was. He knew only that Marian had missed her footing one day when the sea was rough and fallen down one of the steep narrow stairs called companionways.

"She landed with her foot twisted under her. She says she really saw the stars people talk about!"

"Did the ship's doctor look at her foot?" Hurok asked.

He had examined it as carefully as he could, but there was no X-ray machine on board. Marian wore a bandage the rest of the trip and rested a good deal.

"But she had promised to sing in the ship's concert," Vehanen said. "She insisted on keeping her promise, and she did not want anyone to know about the accident, so she stood up to sing. I know it was hard for her."

All sorts of possibilities were flashing through Hurok's mind while Vehanen was talking. It might be nothing but a minor sprain that would heal in a few days. In that case, Marian was wise to keep it a secret. On the other hand, it might be more serious. It might even be a broken bone! In that case the concert would have to be postponed.

There is nothing a manager hates worse than a postponed concert. It is costly in time and in money. Tickets must be returned and money refunded. New posters and programs must be printed. Advertising must be run all over again. It is difficult to persuade the managers of concert halls to change a date without paying a high penalty fee. At this stage of the season, it might not be possible to get another open date at Town Hall. Critics who had made plans to come on the first date might have another commitment on the second. And finally a postponement started rumors, none of them complimentary. People always suspected that whatever reason was given, the real one was a lack of confidence—"singer's nerves."

Still, what had to be, had to be! If there must be a change of dates, the sooner, the better!

Hurok gave Marian time to get home to Philadelphia and have a good night's sleep. Then he telephoned her.

"How are you feeling?" he asked.

There was a tiny pause.

"Fine," said the beautiful, velvety voice.

"Have you seen a doctor?"

There was a longer pause.

"You mean—?"

"About your foot."

"Yes." There was relief in Marian's voice. "I was just trying to decide what to say to you. There is a broken bone. I am wearing a cast."

It was Hurok who made the little pause this time. He tried to keep his voice very calm, as if this sort of news were an every day occurrence.

"Do you want to postpone?" he asked, and held his breath while he waited for her answer.

"No," she said. "I should like to go on as we planned, if you are willing to."

He could have cheered! Instead he asked whether she was still suffering much pain.

"Not now that the foot is all encased in plaster," she said. "I've tried standing on it, too. If I put my weight on the other foot, and lean a little on the piano with my elbow, I can manage very well." But there was one thing

[36]

that had been troubling her as she tried to plan the concert. "How am I to make my entrance? I don't want to be wheeled on, or to hobble out on crutches."

Hurok thought a moment and then had an inspiration.

"Suppose we keep the front curtains closed. You come out any way you want. Get all set. We pull the curtains, and there you are!"

"That's all right, I suppose," she said, a little uncertainly. "Unless it will seem too dramatic. Pulling the front curtain isn't customary at a concert, is it?"

"We could make an announcement and explain."

"No," she said firmly. "I think it would be better not to say anything. If it is possible, I should like not to have anyone know."

"It's possible if you stay quietly at home till you come up for the concert," Hurok said.

"I shall. But you must warn Kosti. He was not to tell anyone, and he did tell you, didn't he?"

Hurok made excuses for Vehanen, but as soon as Marian had hung up, he called him on the phone, told him the news, and spoke very sternly about how important it was to keep Marian's injury a secret.

"I'll do as you say," Vehanen promised. "But I don't understand you Americans. In my country it would be considered much to Marian's credit that she goes on in spite of such a handicap."

"We don't want credit," Hurok said dryly. "We want praise for her voice. Never mind her courage!"

"Will the critics praise her voice less because she has courage?"

[37]

"That's how it works out. People will be making up their minds what to think. They hear what they are expecting to hear—critics the same as audience. If they know she is in pain, they will hear it. Someone will write a column about how a broken bone in the toe affects the high or the low notes of the voice! Believe me! I know these critics!"

The secret was kept very well. (Not perfectly, as it turned out afterwards, but with results quite different from those Hurok had predicted.)

Marian came to New York the day before the concert for a press conference in Hurok's office. When the reporters arrived, she was already seated behind the big desk, which completely concealed her feet. No one saw the big, clumsy, plaster cast. No one could have guessed from her manner that there was anything bothering her, not even normal day-before-concert nerves.

Hurok had seen many performers under stress. He thought he knew all there was to know about the artistic temperament, its strengths and its weaknesses. But he had never seen poise like Marian's. If hers was not a fighting spirit, it was just as tough and courageous in another way.

Such a spirit did not need luck, he told himself. It made its own.

But for all that, when the hour finally came and the crowd began arriving, Hurok was pacing the lobby and corridors of Town Hall, smoking and scowling and growling.

"You're making everybody else nervous," Mae Frohman told him. "Go for a walk. Get a cup of coffee. Read a newspaper. Just don't go backstage where you can upset Marian and Kosti."

He tried all these suggestions in turn. None worked very well, but somehow the time passed. The hall filled. The warning bell rang. He took his place in the box he had reserved for himself and his staff—if any of them had time to sit and listen.

There was a hush in the hall. If there had been talk about the curtains, which few of the concertgoers had ever seen closed, it was all over now. A few throats were cleared, lest a cough spoil the music that was to come. Two late-comers were making nuisances of themselves, crawling over the knees of others to reach their seats in the center of the fourth row. A few programs rustled.

Hurok glanced at his own program to remind himself what Marian had chosen as her opening song. It was Handel's *"Begrüssung,"* a song of greeting. A little prickle of shock ran over him. That was a song to challenge the most experienced performer singing under the happiest conditions!

It began with a long, long note that was supposed to swell very gradually from soft to loud, without a break or a quaver. As simple and as difficult a feat as a dancer standing on the pointed toes of one foot without trembling for second after second!

Anybody but Marian Anderson would have made changes in the program to make things easier, to make up for the special strain she was under. But that was not her way. Having decided to go on with the concert, she was going on as if nothing had happened. Her way of overcoming obstacles that fate put in her path was simply to ignore them.

The tall gold curtains were drawn apart. There in the center of the stage was Kosti, seated at the piano, straight-backed and distinguished in his black tailcoat and white tie. Standing near him in the satiny curve of the grand piano was Marian. Only someone very familiar with her platform manners would have noted anything unusual in the fact that she was standing so close to the instrument that she was actually touching it. Hurok looked at her feet, but they were hidden by the folds of the black and gold gown. Not a sliver of white plaster showed beneath it.

There was a polite round of applause from the audience—no more, no less than there would have been if singer and pianist had walked out and taken their places.

Marian bowed graciously and waited for quiet.

The great dark eyes were closed now, the face lifted, and very, very softly the opening note sounded. It came like the light of a dawn, so slowly that it was hard to be sure when it actually began. It swelled like light, stronger and stronger, steady and pure.

Was the tone perfectly free? Hurok was not sure. Perhaps because he knew too much, he imagined that he heard a shadow of caution. But no one else would catch it. The audience was tremendously impressed. One could almost feel its great collective breath being held while Marian's poured out . . . endlessly . . .

There!

The voice soared into melody at last. The audience gave a sigh of delight and approval.

[40]

Relaxing a little, Hurok settled back to indulge in the rare pleasure of enjoying a concert he had arranged.

But not for long. Soon his eyes were roving restlessly over the faces of those listeners he could see. He recognized a few professional singers. He thought he could read approval and admiration in their expressions, but it was hard to be sure. Professionals were masters at covering their reactions.

Ah, but wait! he thought. There was something coming that would startle them out of their reserve. The group of Schubert songs on the program included the famous dialogue, "Death and the Maiden." Marian's tremendous range and her natural dramatic flair made her interpretation of this song something unforgettable. One actually heard two voices: the maiden's, high and clear and touchingly innocent; the other so dark and deep that it seemed the grave itself was speaking.

Not even the most jealous rival or the most blasé critic would be able to resist that song if Marian was at her best. Without thinking, Hurok looked toward that part of the orchestra floor where the critics were customarily seated—the fifth, sixth, seventh and eighth rows on both sides of the center aisle. He searched out one after another of the men on whose reaction so much depended. They were all in their places—No!

Where was Olin Downes, the critic of the New York *Times?*

Someone else was in his seat, not Downes! Hurok knew him too well to be mistaken even at this distance and in this light. He slipped out of the box and hurried down the corridors looking for Mae or Gerry Goode. He found them together.

"Who's here from the *Times?*" he asked.

"Howard Taubman."

"Taubman? Oh! The young fellow—"

"The young man who writes so well," Mae said. "You liked his reviews last summer when—"

"Never mind last summer!" Hurok interrupted. "Where is Downes? Why didn't he come himself?"

"He's probably gone to the opera," Goode said. "Flagstad is singing tonight in *Tristan and Isolde.*"

Of course! He had forgotten! That was the second piece of bad luck. He had pushed it out of his mind while he worried about the first.

The most popular soprano of the Metropolitan was appearing on this of all nights in her most famous role! Something else he could not have foreseen or avoided, for opera schedules are not announced far in advance and are subject to change without notice. It was just another of the hazards of show business, like sudden blizzards or financial panics.

Hurok had hoped the critics would feel that Marian's concert was more newsworthy, because she was more of an unknown quantity. (Critics are, after all, supposed to be newspapermen and therefore interested in the new.) Many had come tonight for just that reason. Some might leave before the end of the concert to catch part of the opera, but they would write their reviews of Marian's homecoming appearance and sign their names. All but the critic from the *Times!*

The *Times* review, the one which mattered most, would be signed by a young man who was known as the "second-string" critic. What did it matter how much he knew about music, how sound his judgment, how well he could write?

The audience was coming out into the lobby now to smoke and chat during the long intermission. Hurok moved among the groups, listening carefully to all that was said.

It was all good. Better than good. Excellent!

Why should he take it so hard that a single individual was or was not among those who were enjoying this evening? Why? Because that was show business!

The fact that Olin Downes had decided not to come, marked this as a "second-string" event. Those without complete confidence in their own judgment would take their cue from this. And there were very few—in his opinion—who had that sort of confidence.

This concert had been jinxed from the start, Hurok told himself gloomily. He ought to have urged Marian to postpone, picked another hall, another date. Or perhaps it was Marian who was jinxed, at least in America. How many times she had stood on the brink of success only to have it come to nothing! Through no fault of her own! Not even because she was darkskinned in a country of fair-skins! Only because the breaks went against her!

Well, a good gambler never whimpers. He had paid a lot of money for this concert. He might as well enjoy it. He squared his shoulders so as not to look as discouraged as he felt, and went back to his box.

Marian had begun the group of spirituals with which she always ended her programs.

As Hurok settled himself in his seat, he sensed that there was a different atmosphere in the hall. He was not sure at first what the difference was.

". . . *crucified my Lord* . . ."

Marian's deep tones throbbed like a church organ, and Hurok saw heads in the front rows bow, as if in prayer.

"*And He never said a mumberlin' word* . . ."

The hall had become a church, a temple! That was the difference. What the audience was responding to was no longer just a concert. It was a religious experience.

He looked toward the stage. Marian's eyes were closed, as they always were. Her face had the masklike quality he had noticed that night in Paris. But it was a different mask now—the image of worshipful adoration.

Then his own eyes closed and his head bowed.

Chapter 4

White Paper

On the morning of the last day of the year 1935, the New York *Times* music page carried a review signed modestly with the initials, H. T.

Gerry Goode and Mae Frohman were bent over his desk, reading it, when Hurok came into his office.

"Take a look at this!" they both said at once.

**MARIAN ANDERSON
IN CONCERT HERE**
Negro Contralto Returns to
New York After 4 Years
Spent in Europe
APPLAUDED AT TOWN HALL

"Good, said Hurok, looking at the headlines only. "But nothing you can quote in the ads."

"Keep reading," Goode said with a smile.

[45]

Let it be said at the outset: Marian Anderson
has returned to her native land one of the great
singers of our time.

"Is that something you could quote in the ads, or
isn't it?"

Hurok grinned. One such sentence was all you needed.
It hardly mattered whose name or initials were signed at
the bottom of the column. That it appeared in the *Times*
was enough.

"Go on," Mae said. "Read the rest of it."

. . . There was no doubt of it, she was mistress of
all she surveyed.

The simple facts are better than superlatives.
. . . Fact one, then, should be the sheer magnif-
icence of the voice itself considered as a musical
instrument. . . . Fact two should be Miss Anderson's musicianship.

"It takes a young man to write like that," said Mae.
"When he gets excited, he doesn't care who knows it!"

"Keep reading," Goode prodded. "You're going to
have to eat crow about something else before you finish."

. . . Here was a woman of poise and sensibility.
The fact that one foot, injured in an accident on
board ship in the voyage home, was encased in a
cast was never permitted to intrude on the listener's consciousness.

So! Young H. T. was a smart reporter as well as a
critic! This was one time Hurok didn't mind being proved
wrong. He would apologize to Kosti Vehanen for his bad
prediction, with pleasure.

"Now read the last paragraph," Mae said. "It's the part I like best."

In the last four years, Europe has acclaimed this tall, handsome girl. It is time for her own country to honor her. . . . If Joe Louis deserves to be an American hero for bowling over a lot of pushovers, then Marian Anderson has the right to at least a comparable standing. Handel, Schubert, and Sibelius are not pushovers. H. T.

"You know something?" Hurok said to Mae, as if he had just made one of his discoveries. "This young man is going places in his profession."

After that it was easy.

He took Carnegie Hall for a concert two weeks after the Town Hall appearance. Every seat was sold. This time Olin Downes did not find another musical event more worthy of his attention. Marian Anderson was the biggest news of the New York season.

If Hurok did not book 15 concerts that first year, it wasn't because he didn't have 15 offers. He picked and chose among many more than that, accepting only those that represented a real step forward for his protegée. He knew that losing a little now would mean gaining a great deal in the long run. It was not even a gamble any more.

He chose to present her only in the best auditorium of any city, as part of the most distinguished concert series, or under the best auspices if it was a special event like a charity benefit. Marian's fee was as high as that of any singer in the country. Managements who presented her on these terms did so well that they wanted her back next season. Newspapers were unanimous in their praise, from coast to coast.

There were complaints from groups that had supported her in her early days, especially the Negro churches and clubs and colleges that could not afford the new fees. They were sure that Marian would understand their problem and make exceptions for them. And so she would have, if it had been up to her.

But by the terms of their agreement, all questions of business were Hurok's to decide. He had one answer to requests for special consideration—one Marian could never have given for herself:

"She has worked hard to deserve her success. Let those who want to hear her work hard too. Get a larger hall. Sell more tickets. Then there will be no problem about the fee."

It was that policy that had triggered this trouble at Constitution Hall.

The committee who arranged the concert series of Howard University made no objection to paying the new fee, although Marian had sung for them at lower ones many times before. They seemed proud that a singer they had helped on her way could now command such a figure. But obviously no hall on the campus was big enough to bring in that amount of money. They went after the one hall in the city of Washington that was.

Hurok was pleased when he heard that this was the plan. An appearance at Constitution Hall carried a certain prestige with it, and he wanted that prestige for Marian. Roland Hayes, who had blazed the trail she was following had sung there once. But since that time, no other Negro had. It was more or less understood that this was a matter of policy. But the policy had been relaxed once. For a star as bright as Marian, why couldn't it be relaxed again?

He would have been proud if it had happened without any trouble. But he would also have been a little surprised. Perhaps, secretly, he would even have been a little disappointed, for an easy victory was an anticlimax after the battle he had just been reliving in his memory, a battle that called out Marian's particular brand of fighting courage, as it had not been called out since her Town Hall performance.

Why was he hesitating about calling on it now?

Gerry Goode and Mae Frohman were still there, waiting for him to make up his mind.

"All right," he said. "Go after the proof you need, Gerry. Talk to Marks Levine. Show him the editorial from the Washington *Herald*. He'll go for that. And put the people at Howard on the alert. Tell them we may have news for them."

A day or two later, another strategy conference was called in the private office.

Gerry Goode had two telegrams.

The first was addressed to Marks Levine. It was from Fred Hand, and it informed Mr. Levine that Constitution Hall would be available for a concert by Paderewski on April 8th or April 10th.

[49]

"It's available for a Polish pianist, but not for an American singer," said Goode dryly, and put down the second telegram.

It was also from Fred Hand, addressed to Mr. Cohen, of the Howard University Concert Series:

NEITHER DATE AVAILABLE FOR CONCERT
BY MARIAN ANDERSON.

"Well, that's that," said Mae. "No one can want any more proof."

"What are you going to do?" Hurok asked Goode. "Release the two telegrams to the newspapers?"

"No. I promised Mr. Levine I'd only use his if I had to—in case anyone challenges our facts."

"Who's going to challenge them if they don't hear about them?"

"I know," Goode said. "That's the problem: how to get a news break."

"I thought you were going to work on the D.A.R. members," Mae said, "and get them to work on their officers to have the policy changed."

"I can't write a letter to every D.A.R. member," Goode reminded her. "I've got to get the story before the whole public. One thing I'd like to do, as a start, is to draw up a fact sheet—what they'd call a 'white paper' in Washington. Get it all down in black and white. Print up a lot of copies. And send one to every city desk, every music critic, every feature writer on every newspaper in the country."

"It won't get printed," Hurok warned him. "Last week's news is ancient history. Especially with what's going on in Europe now."

"This is just for background," Goode said. "We still need a news peg. But we'll find one."

"I read something in one of the papers today," Mae remembered. "Lawrence Tibbett sent a protest to the D.A.R. I meant to clip it for you. It was really very good."

She started to leaf through the papers on the desk, looking for the item.

"That's what I mean," Hurok said. "It was good, but you can't find it! Now, if Lawrence Tibbett would persuade his fellow members of the Musicians Guild to refuse to appear in Constitution Hall, that would make news!"

"You're probably kidding," said Gerry Goode, "but something like that just might happen before we get through."

"Fine," said Hurok. "Go get up your white paper, in case it does. And by the way, I wasn't kidding."

Chapter 5

Furore

I t was the end of February—a bright, brisk San Francisco day.

Marian was on her way to practice with Kosti when a newspaper headline caught her eye:

**FURORE OVER
MRS. F.D.R.'S
RESIGNATION!**

She was interested in anything that had to do with President Roosevelt's wonderfully warm, keen, active wife. Marian and thousands of other Americans made a habit of reading Mrs. Roosevelt's syndicated newspaper column, "My Day." But Marian had hardly seen a newspaper since she started on this tour. The headline reminded her that she had missed "My Day" for weeks.

If she hadn't already passed the newsstand, she would have bought a paper. Before she saw another stand, she was at the concert hall.

[52]

She meant to ask Kosti about the news story, for he was interested in all things American and a much more faithful newspaper reader than she. But Kosti was not feeling well that afternoon, and Marian forgot the headline in her concern for him.

At the beginning of the season, Kosti had warned Marian that he might not be able to finish the tour. He had been ill, and his doctor said that unless medicines and a careful diet cured him, his gall bladder might have to be removed. For a while he felt better, but now he was having trouble again.

"It's not serious," he assured Marian. "And if we get down to work, I'll forget all about it."

They got to work, and worked so hard that both lost track of time. Marian had some shopping to do. Dinner was to be early, at her own request, because this was a performance night. There was less than an hour in which she wanted to do all the errands that she had saved for this afternoon.

As she passed the little room where the stage doorman stayed, she heard someone inquiring for her. It was a man whose voice she did not recognize. Under other circumstances, she would have stopped to see what he wanted. But now she was in a hurry.

She smiled at the doorman over the stranger's shoulder, put her finger to her lips, and slipped out into the darkening twilight.

Dinner that evening was unusually quiet and pleasant, with only her host and hostess at the table.

It was one of the hardships of touring in a country where Negroes are not treated like other citizens that Marian could not always have this sort of relaxed meal before her performance. If she was staying in a hotel, she always took supper in her room, either alone, or with Kosti, and—if he happened to be with them—Isaac Jofe, Hurok's traveling representative.

Unfortunately, in some cities there was no hotel that would rent her a room. There were others in which an exception was made so grudgingly that she preferred not to accept the "favor." Marian had learned that she could not sing well if her mind and spirit were troubled by the feeling of being unwelcome.

Fortunately, there were always people—old friends, or strangers who became new friends—who welcomed her into their homes as if it was a privilege to have her. The drawback was that so often her hosts wanted to share that privilege, and the best time to do it was at a dinner party before the concert. Marian never babied herself before she was to sing, but it was hard to have to meet and make conversation with new people just when she wanted to gather her energy for the task ahead.

She was grateful for the thoughtfulness of her San Francisco hosts, and she thanked them for it. What she didn't realize till later was that they had done more than protect her from new people. They protected her from the news, which they had read but guessed that she had not. The unusual quiet at the table was a conspiracy of silence.

Not till the concert was over was the silence broken, broken with a bang!

Backstage, Marian stood as usual to greet those who came to congratulate her. Tonight, however, her friends and well-wishers were pushed out of the way by a phalanx of newspapermen, including the man she had eluded at the stage door earlier in the day.

"What do you think about the ban?"

"How do you feel about the D.A.R.?"

"Do you expect to sing in Washington anyway?"

"Do you think the school board will give in?"

"Would you be willing to sing in the auditorium of an all-white school?"

"Have you seen a copy of the petition?"

The questions flew at her like leaves in a storm wind. She had no idea what most of them meant. She did know that there was a Washington date on her schedule. It was still several weeks away. She remembered none of the details.

(There was nothing unusual about such details being left off the schedule as it was given her when she left New York. Final arrangements were seldom made so far in advance. The Hurok office sent bulletins along from time to time, filling in exact time and place, or making changes as they came up.)

"Didn't you know Constitution Hall had a Jim Crow policy?" someone asked.

Marian felt as if a cold hand had been laid on her heart. Kosti was at her elbow now, explaining to her quietly that her concert had been banned at Constitution Hall, that efforts to move it to the auditorium of a Washington high school had also been unsuccessful. There had been a good deal of publicity about protests to both the D.A.R. and the Washington school board.

She stopped listening.

Only once or twice in her life had such a numbing cold gripped her. Marian was remembering the first time . . . remembering it vividly, though it had happened when she was still in her mid-teens. . . .

Chapter **6**

Beginning

S he had wanted to go to a music school—a conservatory, where not only music, but everything there was to know about music, was taught: its history; the lives of great composers; what they had written, not only for the voice but for instruments and orchestra; the music of other civilizations —Indian, African, Chinese; and the languages in which many of the songs she most admired were written.

There was a conservatory in Philadelphia, only a streetcar ride from the neighborhood in which she had lived all her life. Nothing held her back from enrolling in it but the matter of money.

Marian didn't know how much it cost, but almost anything would be too much, for every cent she earned in those days went to help her mother. Mrs. Anderson was struggling to make a living for herself and her daughters. As the oldest, Marian felt it was up to her to help, and she

[57]

gladly contributed the small fees she earned by her singing. But many of her friends thought this was not enough, that she ought to forget about singing and take any steady job she could find.

That was what her mother had done.

She had been a school teacher in Virginia before she came up to Philadelphia to marry Marian's father. When his death left her with three orphan girls to support, she was determined to do it without taking charity, even from the family. She wasted no time trying to get her teacher's credential transferred to another state. She simply went out and took the first jobs she could find—hard, tiring, poorly paid domestic work.

She had been doing it for five years now, years that seemed longer than they were. It was hard to remember when they had not been so poor, to remember the old, happier times and the father that had made them happier. Marian could, a little better than her sisters, but even for her it was hard.

She remembered her father as a very big man, and very kind. He was not as well-educated as her mother, but he worked hard, and took pride in his ability to provide for his family. While he lived there was always plenty of food in the house, and it was always their own house, even though it was small and without many of the conveniences other people enjoyed. There were little treats, like new bonnets for each of the little girls every Easter, bonnets their father picked out himself and brought home.

There was even a piano for Marian. It wasn't new and hadn't been very fine when it was, but it was good enough for picking out melodies at first, and later on for Marian to accompany herself when she sang.

Her father was not especially musical, but he was the one that opened the channel through which music poured so strongly into her early life. Mr. Anderson belonged to the Union Baptist Church, and he began to take Marian there before she was six. (Marian's mother was a Methodist, and her grandfather Anderson called himself a Black Jew. He worshipped on Saturdays instead of Sundays, in a synagogue instead of a church. But Grandmother Anderson was a strong Baptist and a strong-willed woman, who saw to it that all her children and her children's children attended her church.)

Mr. Anderson had many official duties, before, during, and after the Sunday morning service. Marian's sisters were still babies and their mother had to stay home with them. But Marian was big enough to walk with her father; so she left when he did in the morning and stayed till he was ready to come home in the early afternoon.

When they got to church, he would take her down to the basement, where the Sunday School classes met. Marian sang and listened to the lesson with the other children. But when that was over, she went upstairs and found herself a place in one of the back pews under the balcony where the choir was seated.

She might not have sat so patiently through the long grown-up services if it hadn't been for the music. The Union Baptist Church was famous for its choir, not only for the quality of its voices, but for the quality—and the variety—of the music they sang. Under the direction of an

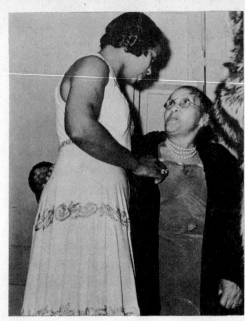

*Marian
and
her mother,
Carnegie Hall,
1947*

unusually able leader, they worked hard and tackled long and difficult works that were not usually attempted by unpaid volunteers.

Marian's taste was formed on the best there was, before her legs were long enough to put her feet on the floor—which was early in her life, for she was a tall child, as she was to be a tall woman. She always sang along with the choir, humming the melody with the sopranos at first. Then, as her ear grew keen enough to distinguish the different voices, she tried humming with the contraltos, or the tenors, or even with the basses, which she could manage by putting it up an octave.

When she was six, her father enrolled her in the junior choir. Not long afterwards, the director, Mr. Robinson, gave her and her friend, Viola Johnson, a duet called

"Dear to the Heart of the Shepherd." The girls practiced it together at home all week, Viola taking the soprano, Marian, the alto part, and they sang it for the Sunday School.

When Marian and her father got home from church that afternoon, they learned that Mr. Robinson had stopped by to say that the girls were to go on practicing, for he wanted them to sing for the congregation next Sunday.

Marian remembered her father trying to look stern to keep his pride from bursting its seams.

"I'm not going to have them singing my child to death," he said.

The year she turned ten, Marian joined the senior choir, and from then on, she sang in both choirs at once. That same year she sang her first solo in public, at a concert her aunt had arranged.

This aunt was also a member of the Union Baptist choir, a woman of great energy, some of which spilled over into other channels. She sang with other groups and took an interest in other churches. One of these was a small, newly-formed congregation that had no building of its own, but met in what had once been a neighborhood store.

Marian's aunt offered to organize a concert to raise funds for the building of a real church, and she asked Marian to take part in the program. Marian said yes without thinking about it. She sang, in those days, whenever and wherever she had a chance—at home, in the homes of friends and relatives, at school, even as she walked along the streets.

She was doing just that one day when she saw a flyer someone had dropped, and picked it up to read it. She saw her own name printed in big letters!

COME AND HEAR THE BABY CONTRALTO!
MARIAN ANDERSON

The world whirled around and came slowly to rest again. She was a different person! A contralto! A singer! A real singer! Like Roland Hayes, who sang every year at the gala concert sponsored by Union Baptist!

She was too happy to be frightened by her new status. She sang that concert as she always sang, out of the fullness of her heart from which music ran like a river whenever she gave it a chance.

Her father was there to hear her.

But not long afterwards there was an accident at the market where he was working. Something fell and hit his head.

At first the doctors told Mr. Anderson that his strength and endurance would pull him through. Later they spoke of a tumor on the brain. As the weather grew colder and the days shorter, he lay quieter and quieter, hardly speaking to any of them.

Then, just before Christmas, he was gone, and everything was changed.

They moved out of their own little house into the one where their Anderson grandparents and their aunt and her children lived. Even that large house was crowded by four extra people; so before long they all moved again.

There were always lots of children in the new house, not only Marian's sisters and cousins, but other children

[62]

whose mothers left them with Grandmother Anderson while they went out to work.

Some days Marian's mother went out to work; other days she brought home clothes to wash and iron. The girls helped by calling for and delivering laundry and collecting the money for it. They ran errands for their grandmother and their aunt. And they went to school.

Marian did all this and sang too. She was still a member of both choirs, which meant choir practice several evenings during the week; and she was an all-purpose substitute for any soloist who failed to show up.

That came about, like many other things connected with her music, so naturally that it was hard to remember how it happened the first time. Someone—perhaps it was one of the male voices—failed to appear at practice. Marian offered to sing the part. She knew them all. She had been listening and humming since she was a tiny girl. Lately she had been taking the music home and picking out the different parts on her piano.

So Mr. Robinson let her fill in during practice. Perhaps she did it many times. She couldn't remember. Eventually there came a Sunday when a soloist sent a message that he or she couldn't be there, when it was too late to get a replacement. By then Marian had proved herself. Mr. Robinson had a choice of trusting her with a solo or skipping the anthem. He trusted her and she did herself proud.

As the years passed, Marian sang many solos, and many different parts. Her voice grew with her and she was growing very fast and very tall. She already towered over her tiny mother. Her voice also towered over those around it.

If she wasn't careful to hold it in, her vibrant contralto would ring out so loud that people in the congregation below heard no one else.

In a different church Marian might have been rebuked and thus discouraged. But the pastor and all the members took great pride in "our Marian." Her pastor Reverend Parks praised her by name from the pulpit when she had done especially well. In this way her name began to become known, to people in her church and neighborhood and city, and to some outside it. For visitors to Philadelphia often made a point of attending a service at Union Baptist just because of the music. Then, when they went home, they could say how its choir compared with their own.

Marian was invited more and more often to sing outside the church by people who had first heard her there. Sometimes on weekends she would sing at as many as three different places in a single evening. Sometimes it was the same song; sometimes a different one at each. Sometimes there was a fee—a few dollars, or only a few dimes, enough to cover her carfare. Sometimes she accompanied herself; sometimes there was someone who played better than she did. Sometimes she sang alone; sometimes in duets with her aunt.

In all those schoolgirl years there was only one experience Marian remembered afterwards as a real leap forward. That was the gala concert where she appeared on the same platform with her idol, Roland Hayes.

Chapter 7

"We Don't Take Colored"

The gala concert had been a highlight of the Union
Baptist's spring program as long as Marian could remember.
Roland Hayes was frequently the featured soloist.

It was from listening to him that Marian first learned
about other sorts of songs than the religious and folk
music she had heard all her life. Hayes sang everything
from operatic arias to spirituals, and he sang in many
languages, especially in German. He was famous for his
interpretations of the lieder (art songs) of Schubert and
Brahms.

Marian was fascinated by these simple sounding but
very difficult pieces of music. But some of the older people
in the congregation occasionally grumbled that they couldn't
understand the words. "If our Marian sang, we could understand her," they would tell Reverend Parks.

[65]

One day he decided to give them what they wanted. He called Marian into his office and asked whether she would like to sing a few selections on the next gala program.

For the first time in her life, Marian was struck with something like stage fright. Not of the audience, who were as familiar to her as her own family. But of Mr. Hayes! The greatest living Negro singer! The first of his race to sing before the crowned heads of Europe! How would he feel about appearing with an unknown school girl?

He couldn't have been kinder. He applauded her songs as warmly as anyone in the audience. When she came back to her seat, he whispered that he would like to have a talk with her and her family before he left the city. And the next day he came to the Anderson house to call.

He talked very seriously about Marian's talent. "She has a great gift, and she ought to have a teacher."

A teacher for singing was a completely new idea to Marian. Like having a teacher for breathing or for praying.

Her mother thanked Mr. Hayes for his interest and explained that there was no money for singing lessons. He too had struggled against poverty; he understood what the problem was. But he did not forget about Marian.

The next time he was in Philadelphia, he visited the house again, this time with a more practical suggestion.

"There is a teacher in Boston named Arthur Hubbard —a fine man who took an interest in me at a time when I stood at a crossroads with my voice. Without his help, I might never have overcome the handicaps that faced me, including the need to make my own and my mother's living while I studied.

[66]

"I have talked to him about Marian, and he is willing to take her as a pupil without charge. She can live in his home and pay her way by helping Mrs. Hubbard with the work of the house."

There was a family conclave that evening, only part of which Marian overheard. That was enough to dash her hopes.

"Send that child all the way to Boston?" asked her grandmother in a tone of shocked indignation. "No girl her age has any business living anywhere except in her own home! Besides, Marian doesn't need a singing teacher. She sings better than any teacher right now."

When Marian's grandmother set her mind for or against something, the family decision was made.

"Don't grieve over it, baby," her mother said to Marian next morning. "If it's the right thing for you, a way will be opened. You just go on doing the best you can in school, and we'll see."

Marian was not doing as well at school as she ought to be. She had already changed high schools once. The first one she attended specialized in commercial courses. She meant to train herself to be a bookkeeper, because she knew of a job she could have if she did. But she did badly in all the commercial courses. She did well in the few music courses that were offered, and she made herself very popular with teachers and students by singing in assemblies. Finally, the principal called her in.

"You really don't belong in a commercial school," she told Marian. "Why don't you let us transfer you to South Philadelphia High School, where you can get a straight college preparatory course?"

"I don't think I'll be going to college," Marian said.

"Even so. There'll be courses that appeal to you more than bookkeeping, and quite a bit more in the way of music."

So Marian changed schools, but even in the new one she was not making much of a record scholastically. She really wasn't a scholar, and besides, she was missing too many classes. For by now she was singing several concerts a month, many of them so far away from Philadelphia that she had to spend one or two nights away from home. She was beginning to earn some money, although the Negro colleges and churches and clubs (to which Mr. Hayes had recommended her) didn't pay very high fees. But it added up to enough to support her, and someone predicted to her grandmother that she would do even better.

"Mark my words, Mrs. Anderson. One day that child is going to be earning as much as $50 a night!"

Her grandmother considered that an exaggeration, but even so she was impressed. That sort of money put singing in a different category. It became a profession, and for a profession one must train.

Not long afterwards, a friend took Marian to sing for Mary Saunders Patterson, a Negro soprano in Philadelphia who had had professional training. When she had listened to Marian, she offered to give her lessons without charge.

A way had opened, just as her mother had predicted.

The first thing Marian learned from Mrs. Patterson was how much there was to learn, beginning with the muscles that made the music, and ending with the vast subject of music itself.

[68]

"You have to learn how to conserve your voice," Mrs. Patterson said. "If you go on using it the way you do now, you'll use it up! You've got to do exercises, like a dancer or a boxer. You have to strengthen your weaknesses and learn to avoid strain. Think of your voice as if it were capital you put in a bank. You don't want to draw out the principal—only the interest."

Never having had much money in a bank, Marian didn't find the example very illuminating at first, but she enjoyed the exercises.

It was Mrs. Patterson who brought up the question of a conservatory.

By this time Marian had been studying with her for some time, had appeared in several of Mrs. Patterson's recitals, and was showing such promise that more and more people seemed to assume she was going to make a career of music.

"You will have to make the decision some day," Mrs. Patterson told her. "If you are going on with your music, you really ought to learn more than I can teach you. You ought to go to a music school."

Marian named the only one she knew of. Did Mrs. Patterson think it was a good one? Was it expensive? Had Marian had enough training to qualify as an entering student?

The teacher hesitated before answering.

"It's very good," she said at last. "I don't know what the tuition is, nor the entrance requirements. But the fall term will be opening soon. Why don't you go down and ask your questions of the registrar?"

[69]

Marian talked it over with her mother and they agreed that it was worth investigating. Even if the fee was high, there must be scholarships. At any rate, there was no use crossing that bridge until they came to it. The first thing was to get the information.

Marian looked up the address in the phone book, and set out one morning fairly early. The more she thought about it, the more exciting an adventure it became. Her imagination transformed the window marked REGISTRAR into a magic gate beyond which lay the kingdom of music in which privileged beings moved in a sort of golden dream . . . the closest thing to the Kingdom of Heaven on earth.

There was a long line of prospective students waiting their turn before that magic gate, but Marian didn't mind. She went to the end of the line, and stood patiently, her heart beating fast and hard at being even this close to her imagined heaven.

Slowly she inched her way forward, until—after almost an hour—she finally stood in front of the little opening in the window. Behind it sat a young girl, a white girl.

"Yes?" she said in a sharp, unfriendly voice.

Marian opened her mouth to ask her question, but the young woman was not looking at her. She was looking past her, at the next person in line.

It was a deliberate piece of rudeness.

Marian was so surprised that she stepped to one side before she had realized it. She stood there, trying to understand what had happened, fighting for calm as person after person came up to the window, asked questions that were answered, requested forms that they were given.

She felt as if her brain had gone numb, so that it could only think very, very slowly. She had lived all her life in a city whose name in Greek meant City of Brotherly Love. She knew perfectly well that not everyone in it loved everyone else like a brother. In her own neighborhood there were people of all colors, all religious and national backgrounds. Some got on together better than others. There were places to which all were not welcome, sometimes for one reason, sometimes for another.

Marian and her family never wanted or needed to go any place where they were not welcome; so these things had never made any deep impression on her. She had heard her mother and her Southern relatives talk about Jim Crow as it was practiced in states to the south, but it had seemed unreal and far away. It didn't seem possible that the sort of cruel exclusion and humiliation she had heard about was being practiced here and now, against her. In Pennsylvania, the promised land of the great Quaker, William Penn! In a place dedicated to something as universal and all-embracing as the art of music!

Now at last the young woman turned to her.

"All right. What do you want?"

The voice stabbed like an icicle. It was worse, somehow, because it came from someone her own age, someone with whom she might have gone to school.

"I would like a registration blank," she said shakily.

"We don't take colored," said the girl and shut the little window with a snap.

[71]

That was the first time her path in life had run into the ice-wall of prejudice. It was not the last time, but it was the hardest to bear because it seemed to her then that she could never find her way over or around the barrier.

She talked to her mother, but to no one else, about it.

"There will be many times in life when you're pulled up short by disappointment," her mother said, not making light of the hurt but secure in her faith that a believer was never dependent on his or her own strength. "If God knows it's right for you, He will raise up someone to be kind. Just trust Him. He will find a way."

Others in the family wouldn't have taken it so calmly. Marian's aunt, if she had known, would have demanded to know whether this was official policy, and if so, why.

But Marian and her mother were much alike in the way they reacted to injustice. They went quietly to the well of their faith to find peace of mind and understanding of their fellow men, even of those who—as Mrs. Anderson put it—"behaved so poorly."

In the years that followed that first disappointment, Marian went often to the well "to be replenished."

There was the first time she rode in a Jim Crow car on a southern railroad. She was on her way to Atlanta where she was to give a concert at Spelman College. She was shocked by the shabby seats and dirty windows in the car to which she changed when the train reached Washington, D.C. But what hurt her even more was the look in the eyes of the people who shared the car with her, the humiliation in some, the resignation in others.

It didn't seem to her that riding in a Pullman car proved anyone was better than anyone else—except in the sense of being able to pay the higher fare. But she saw that accepting second-class treatment of any kind did something very destructive to a person's self-respect.

There were other trials: from the many times she had to sit up all night on a train because there was no berth for a Negro and then sing a concert the next afternoon, to taxi drivers who would not take her and her suitcases from the station to the place she was to stay.

If she had let all these things anger her, she would have had little heart for her work, and it was her work that saved her from anger. She learned to turn to it with redoubled energy after each rebuff. (That was what she did after the rebuff at the conservatory. She went on with her singing lessons, practiced harder than ever.) For she was not cut out to be a fighter for rights, neither her own nor anyone's else. She was cut out to be a singer.

That was all that concerned her, and it concerned her completely. It shaped and gave meaning to her whole life. . . .

"How do you feel about the ban on your Washington concert?"

A reporter's question forced her back to the present. They were all waiting for her answer, pencils poised.

"I am shocked," she said slowly, carefully. "I have sung in the capitals of many other countries. I'm shocked that it should be impossible for me to sing in the capital of my own. . . ."

[73]

Reporters surrounded her.

There was a quick scurrying of pencils across note-books, as they all took her words down.

Why, Marian wondered, were they all so interested? This was not the first time a Negro had met with rejection in the United States. Most instances went unreported. Why was this one news?

"How do you feel about Mrs. Roosevelt's action?"

"Do you know her personally?"

"What has Mrs. Roosevelt to do with this?" Marian asked in astonishment.

"You mean to say you don't know?"

"She's resigned from the D.A.R.!"

"Don't you read her column?"

"Here! Have a look!"

[74]

Someone handed her a newspaper, already two days old. It was folded open to the feature page, where Mrs. Roosevelt's face smiled up from the heading on her column.

Marian ran her eye quickly down the text. It seemed to be the usual, straightforward account of the events, private and public, and the thoughts that filled a day of America's busy First Lady. There was a paragraph marked with heavy pencil, which she had to read twice:

I have been debating in my mind for some time, a question which I have had to debate with myself once or twice before in my life. . . . if you belong to an organization and disapprove of an action which is typical of a policy, should you resign or is it better to work for a changed point of view within the organization? In the past, when I was able to work actively in any organization to which I belonged, I have usually stayed in until I had at least made a fight. . . . But in this case I belong to an organization in which I can do no active work. They have taken an action which has been widely talked of in the press. To remain as a member implies approval of the action and therefore, I am resigning.

The organization was not named, or its action reported. Marian could have read the column and never known that it referred to her.

But everyone else had known.

This was why the reporters were so excited. Everything about Mrs. Roosevelt made news. Front-page news, nationally and—in this case—internationally!

"Maybe you haven't seen what your manager has said either!" One of the reporters read aloud from a different paper, "Let the walls of Constitution Hall tremble at one of the most shocking violations of constitutional rights which I have ever experienced in my twenty-five years as an impresario in America. . . . All my efforts to have the ban lifted have been futile, and what is worse, the infection has spread, for now the Board of Education in Washington has refused the use of Central High School Auditorium.

"But at least in the open square, where I plan to have Miss Anderson sing, she will find the air freer to breathe!"

"What about this open square, Miss Anderson? Are you going to give a concert across the street from Constitution Hall?"

"I know nothing about any such plan," she managed to say, more calmly than she felt. "All arrangements are made by Mr. Hurok."

Chapter 8

Under Fire

Day by day the excitement grew instead of slacking off as Marian had expected it would. Mrs. Roosevelt's resignation seemed to touch off a chain of little explosions, some inside, some outside the D.A.R.

There were other resignations, some of which had happened before Mrs. Roosevelt's but were only publicized afterwards. One of the first was that of the wife of the singing teacher with whom Marian had studied longest: Giuseppe Boghetti of Philadelphia. Another was Dr. Elsie Mitchell of California, one of the only two life members of the organization. Another was Josephine Truslow Adams, of the famous Adams family of Massachusetts. She and some of her fellow-members set up a D.A.R. of their own with a policy of no discrimination. For a week or so there was speculation as to which set of Daughters would be officially recognized by the Sons of the American Revolution. In the end, the old guard won out.

It was the same in the D.A.R. itself. Although there were protests from some state chapters, the national board voted to support their officers' action. But individuals and some fairly large groups found ways to make their disagreement known.

In one small Texas city, for instance, the local chapter ordered a block of 200 seats for Marian's concert. Requests were received from the Junior Daughters for concerts by Marian next season under their sponsorship.

Among the comic sidelights to the serious controversy was the tempest over a tea party.

Every spring there was a gathering of D.A.R. officers in Washington, and since the election of Mr. Roosevelt put a Daughter in the White House, it had become customary to invite the visiting ladies to an afternoon reception and tea. Arrangements for this year had been made before the trouble began.

Would the invitation be cancelled in view of the new circumstances? Would the ladies come, or stay away? Would Mrs. Roosevelt be there to welcome them in person, or would a substitute hostess preside? The newspapers had fun with these questions for a week or so before they discovered that Mrs. Roosevelt planned to be in Seattle at that time because her daughter was expecting a baby. No one could make anything controversial out of that.

All this time protests from people in every walk of life were arriving at D.A.R. headquarters, with copies sent to the newspapers, which printed most of them. Such famous singers as Kirsten Flagstad and Grace Moore; the famous conductor, Serge Koussevitsky of the Boston Symphony; such composers as Deems Taylor; and many others were quoted in strong statements of disapproval. Jascha Heifetz, the world-famous violinist, played a concert in Constitution Hall and was asked afterwards how he felt about it.

"Really uncomfortable," he confessed. "To think that this very hall in which I played today has been barred to a great singer made me ashamed."

There was a story to the effect that Local 77 of the Musicians Union was considering a boycott of the hall by all its members.

Not only figures from the world of music wanted to be heard on the question. Actors and churchmen and politicians and educators—everyone in public life, it seemed, had an opinion to express. They were all on the same side until Westbrook Pegler, newspaper columnist, wrote a defense of the D.A.R. and spoke slightingly of a "hitherto obscure Negro singer named Marian Anderson," who—he implied—was enjoying a lot of undeserved, free publicity.

That started another storm.

Venerable conductor-composer, Walter Damrosch, gave his opinion that, "This lady is one of the greatest artists of song that we have."

Even editors in the Deep South expressed their scorn of the ban. In Jackson, capital city of Mississippi, the *News* carried the following item:

They wouldn't let Marian Anderson, negro contralto, possessor of the world's most marvelous voice,

sing in Continental [*sic*] Hall at Washington, but we have no such foolish racial prejudice down here in the South. Marian Anderson will sing in the municipal auditorium at Memphis on March 30, and there will be as many white folks as negroes present to hear her.

Meanwhile, on another battlefront in the same war, the representatives of Howard University were protesting the refusal of the District of Columbia Board of Education to permit the use of Central High School's auditorium for the concert on April 9.

The Board had given as its reason the fact that Miss Anderson's fee was too high to make "appropriate" the use of a "free" public facility. But everyone knew that the real reason was that Washington schools were segregated. Central High was all-white. It would be a breach of Jim Crow's unwritten law to let a Negro contralto sing from its auditorium stage to an audience that would contain many Negro listeners.

Here was a deeper issue. People who felt strongly one way or the other about segregation in public schools—especially in the nation's capital—took up their weapons and rushed into the fight.

On the day Heifetz played in Constitution Hall, there was a picket line in front of the Board of Education. And in Central High School itself, students were arguing the question, on which their opinion had not so far been requested by anyone.

A student named Leon Smith, one of the editors of the *Central Bulletin,* summed up his side in an editorial, that was set up in type in the school print shop under the headline:

REFUSAL TO NEGRO ARTIST
IS RACE INTOLERANCE

When proofs of the forthcoming *Bulletin* were pulled, one copy was sent, as usual, to the principal. He read the editorial and decided it would be wiser not to have the students publicly criticizing the school board. The editorial did not appear in that week's *Bulletin.* But not all the proof copies were destroyed, as Principal Hoover expected them to be.

The school board received about that time a petition bearing thousands of signatures that had been collected by the Marian Anderson Protest Committee. This was a brand new organization, but already its steering committee consisted of representatives of 24 other organizations, some of them national. The petition protested the Board's action as "contrary to the spirit of democracy and a backward step in the development of interracial good will in the District of Columbia." The Board was urged to reconsider.

Just to make things more complicated, while these people were criticizing the school board for refusing the Howard University request, some other people were criticizing Howard for the way the request was worded.

What bothered them was that the tone was so modest. It asked for the use of Central High "for a specific concert by a specific artist." Charles Houston, attorney for the university, stated frankly that they were not challenging the policy of school segregation at that time. Some people

[*81*]

felt that it ought to be challenged, and that this was a good time to begin.

George Schuyler, who wrote for the Pittsburgh *Defender* and was syndicated in Negro papers all over the North, and others used such scathing expressions as "handkerchief heads" and "Uncle Toms" in referring to the Howard authorities. Pressure from this side was growing stronger all the time, and made compromise more and more difficult.

And compromise was what the school board finally decided to offer.

Its president, Dr. F. W. Ballou, thought he had found a formula that would satisfy the demands of one side and calm the fears of the other. The Howard University officials were informed that they could have Central High School, but for this concert only! It must be clear that this was a special exception. It was not to be taken as a precedent. To make perfectly sure that both sides understood this, the university officials were to agree never to ask such a "favor" again. Not for Marian Anderson or anyone else.

By this time even the most conservative members of the Negro community were in no mood to sign what someone called "a blank check on the future."

The request to the Board of Education was restated to ask for the use of Central High School Auditorium without any qualifications. On that basis, it was again turned down. Instead of compromising the difference, the effect of all this was to sharpen it.

More headlines. More comment by prominent citizens. More editorials. And more discussion in the lobbies of the Capitol, where senators and congressmen were beginning to take sides.

Congress had a particular interest in all this because the District of Columbia has no city or state government. Congress makes the rules under which the District's public affairs are conducted. Some people were saying that Constitution Hall was a "public" building because it was operated tax free by a "patriotic organization." Whether or not one agreed with that, there was no questions about the use of public schools being Congressional business, if Congress chose to make it so.

Someone said it was high time there was an investigation of the question of the separation of Negro and white students, and for that matter, of race relations as a whole in the capital city.

Through all this excitement, Marian and Kosti were continuing with their tour.

They had gone down the West Coast, turned back toward the East, and worked their way half across the country when Kosti suddenly became very ill.

He was flown to Washington for surgery. Marian had to decide whether to cancel the rest of the tour or find a substitute who could take over almost without rehearsal.

"Don't cancel," Kosti begged when she said good-bye to him at the airport. "Change the program, if you must. Cut out the things that are not familiar to whoever takes my place. But give the concerts you have promised. There are only three more."

Marian said she would try.

The Hurok office in New York was already on the lookout for a substitute pianist, and within a few hours they phoned to say that a highly qualified young man named Franz Rupp was willing to take the next plane to St. Louis and meet Marian on the morning of her concert.

While she waited, Marian went over her whole repertory, preparing to make the sort of changes Kosti had suggested. It was only fair to make no unnecessary demands on her new partner. There would only be a few hours for them to work together, to get used to each other, and set the signals by which a singer gives an accompanist his cues— signals that had become second nature to Marian, so that she had a hard time calling them to her conscious mind.

The best thing to do was to choose songs with which Mr. Rupp was familiar, so that he didn't also have to read the music at sight. Marian had plenty of possible alternatives for any song or group of songs, but she found it hard to think of using them. This program, like all her programs, was the result of hours of thought and discussion, of trial and error. Kosti had helped her to think of the building of a program as a problem in architecture: getting just the right balance between music of different moods, between new works and old ones, between complex, sophisticated forms and simpler ones.

Any change at all would disturb that balance.

Besides, she had no way of knowing which songs would be unfamiliar to her new pianist, or which alternatives would be less so. She decided to put the choice up to him. She would do the adjusting—and do her best to conceal her uneasiness about it.

Franz Rupp accompanying Marian Anderson

Her first impression of Franz Rupp was of a small, compactly built young man who made her feel even taller than usual by contrast. He was as different from Kosti as could be—in every way but the one that mattered at the moment.

He looked over the program as originally planned and said there would be no need to make any change in it.

Marian could hardly believe her luck, but a single run-through convinced her that he was right. He was a fine and an experienced accompanist. The concert could go off as planned. Meanwhile she had called Washington and learned that Kosti was resting very comfortably after his operation.

It was almost too good to be true.

[85]

Mr. Rupp stayed with Marian for the two remaining concerts on her schedule, and the season was over at last.

It had not been an easy one and Marian was glad to be on her way home. But she felt that she ought to make one stop on the way: in Washington, to make sure that Kosti was coming along as well as his cheerful little notes said he was.

There was nothing else on her mind as she sat in her compartment looking out the window at the first signs of spring on the Virginia countryside. There was a knock at her door. She called "Come in," expecting the porter with a clothes brush. But it was Gerald Goode, the press agent from the Hurok office.

"What are you doing on this train?" she asked in astonishment. "Have you been on long?"

"No," he said. "I just got on. I thought I'd better warn you before you pull into Washington. Every reporter who isn't waiting for you in the station is waiting in the lobby of Vehanen's hospital."

"Has something happened to Kosti?"

"No, it's you. What's happened is the Marian Anderson Protest Meeting that's coming up on Sunday."

"Protest Meeting!"

She sounded so horrified that Goode couldn't keep from smiling.

"I guess I've started at the wrong end of the story," he said, "but maybe it would be better if I didn't start at the right end till we have more time. Besides, if you don't know what's going on, you can say so to the reporters. They may not believe you, but you'll feel better if it's true."

Marian agreed. She had deliberately avoided knowing what was going on in Washington these last few weeks, because it made it easier to avoid questions. She suspected that the situation was complicated and changing so rapidly that anything she said was apt to add to the confusion, even if it was not misquoted or misinterpreted.

Mr. Goode hadn't exaggerated either the size of the crowd of reporters or their eagerness to question her. But with his help and her armor of innocence she managed to fend them off and inch her way toward the car that was waiting to drive her to the hospital.

She had her hand on the door handle when one reporter asked a question that could not be answered by her formula of "I really don't know."

"Miss Anderson, do you regret your decision to return to America?"

It was spoken in English but with a strong Scandinavian accent. Marian turned to the man who had asked it. He bowed and identified himself as the representative of a Swedish press service. He was respectful and friendly and she didn't want to answer him sharply. But his question implied something that bothered her.

"I'm afraid I don't understand," she said. "There was never any decision to return to America, because I never had any idea of living anywhere else."

The man was too polite to contradict her, but he was obviously not convinced.

"It is said in my country that your friends in Stockholm urged you to make your home with us, where you were honored. A singer's home must be where her voice finds its home. Is it not so? It is said that you would have stayed in Sweden if you could have persuaded your family to join you."

"No," said Marian. "It wasn't like that at all. . . ."

And yet, in a way, it had been.

She had never made such a decision, but there was a time—she could see it now looking back—when something almost like that had happened without her intending it.

For it is true that any professional's home is where he can practice that profession. Marian had known before she was out of high school that she wanted to be a professional singer, to make a career of her music, to give her life to training and using her gift of song.

She had never turned from the path she set her foot on then, and it had led her very far from home before it finally doubled back. . . . Perhaps, if it had not been for a certain lucky accident, it might never have made that final turn . . . .

Chapter 9

"You Will Sing Anywhere"

The first step on the path was an audition with Giuseppe Boghetti, a professional teacher of professional singers, who had his main studio in Philadelphia, and another in New York.

Even to secure a hearing from such a personage, much less be accepted as his pupil, was a feat. On her own, Marian might not have attempted it. But a lady who heard her sing at a school assembly offered to arrange it for her. The lady's name was Lisa Roma, and she was herself a pupil of Mr. Boghetti's.

Grateful as Marian was for Miss Roma's offer, she wasn't sure she could afford the lessons, even if Mr. Boghetti was willing to give them. She had been earning more money, giving programs quite regularly in Philadelphia and nearby cities, and now and then making longer journeys, like the one to Atlanta. But she was beginning to feel that her mother ought to stop working altogether.

Mrs. Anderson no longer did work in people's homes, but her job as a cleaning woman at Wanamaker's Department Store was hard and unpleasant, too great a strain on a woman who had already overdrawn her account of physical strength. With all three of her girls in high school, the expenses Mrs. Anderson had to meet out of her small paychecks were greater than ever. She was determined that all three girls must stay in school till they graduated. With Marian's earnings they could manage. But not with Marian's earnings minus a singing teacher's fee.

"It doesn't seem right to go for an audition without having any idea how I'm going to get the money," Marian said to Miss Roma.

"Why don't you talk it over with your friends at the church where you sing?"

Marian did, and all of them—her pastor, the choir director, and some of the older members who had been friends of her father's and her grandmother's—told her the same thing.

"See if he'll take you. If he will, that means you've got as much talent as we believe. We'll find a way to get the money for you. Just you go and try."

Mr. Boghetti was a short, stocky man with a very gruff manner.

He began the audition by telling Marian that he had more pupils than he wanted, and was anxious to get rid of some, not to take on any more.

"I am listening to you only as a favor to Lisa," he said. "I tell you ahead of time, so you will not be disappointed, I will not be your teacher."

With that, he sat down at the piano to play her accompaniment.

Marian had chosen an old spiritual, a song she had known since she was a child. She could have sung it in her sleep, which was a good thing, for Mr. Boghetti's rudeness had upset her a little.

She took a deep breath, closed her eyes and began.

"Deep River, my home is over Jordan . . ."

The song made its own magic curtain that shielded her from everything except the music. The notes of the piano came through, true and strong. Mr. Boghetti might be unfriendly as a person, but as an accompanist he was a true partner.

". . . to cross over into camp ground."

The last note was touched gently, almost reluctantly, and died out. There was silence. Marian opened her eyes.

"I would like to hear you sing a scale," Mr. Boghetti said abruptly.

He sounded a note and commanded her to follow him up. Up, up, as high as she could go, and then down again. Down, down, lower than she had ever sung before.

"I will teach you," he said.

Marian looked at him in surprise. He was still scowling fiercely.

"You will study with me two years. At the end of that time, you will be able to sing anywhere! Town Hall! Carnegie Hall! The Academy of Music! Even the Opera!"

He went on barking out short, sharp little phrases, naming the fee he would charge, the days of the week and the hours he would assign to her lessons, the time he would expect her to practice.

"We will begin next Tuesday. It is the first of the month. Agreed?"

"But I can't," Marian got in a breathless word at last. "I have to get the money first."

Mr. Boghetti glared, first at her, then at Lisa Roma, as if to ask why she had brought him a pupil who couldn't afford the lessons she was asking for. Didn't she know he made his living by teaching? Did she expect him to re-arrange his whole schedule to accommodate her friend and teach her for nothing too?

"I'm sure the problem can be solved," said Lisa, quite unruffled. "Marian has many friends. Give us a week or so. We'll find a way."

The way that was found was a gala concert in the Union Baptist Church. Nothing could have been more ap-propriate, for it was here that Marian had first used the voice that was now to be trained for greater usefulness. It was here she had been "discovered" by Roland Hayes, and he was to sing at her concert.

Marian would never forget that evening. It bound her with cords of love and gratitude to a whole group of people —her people! Not only her family and the friends whose faces she recognized in the audience, but people she had never seen before, strangers who came to hear her and to contribute their bit toward her needs. Strangers, who stood for all the hundreds, the thousands, who were to come to her for inspiration, and were to give her inspiration to travel far and climb high!

More than $600 was collected at that concert, a lot of money for people who had a need to match every nickel or dime they earned. What was even more important to Marian was the knowledge that this was only the beginning. It was the founding of an invisible treasury to which she could go again and again, whenever she had to.

After this, she could never forget that her gift did not belong to her alone.

Mr. Boghetti started the first lesson in the same brusque tone he had used at the audition.

"You remember the scale you sang? It was uneven. Some tones were strong. Others not. We will work on the weak ones.

"Now! Tell me how you make a tone."

Marian had never thought about "making" a tone before her lessons with Mrs. Patterson. She just opened her mouth and let the breath pour out in song. But her first teacher had taught her to focus, or "point" her voice toward a particular spot—a far corner of the room in which she sang.

She explained this to Mr. Boghetti, but he made fun of so simple a notion.

"What if you must sing in a room that has no corners? Many concert halls are circular!"

Marian had no answer.

"You make the tone in your head," he said, and explained that there were air chambers in the bone of the skull that must be made to vibrate before anything happened in the air outside.

He struck E flat on the piano.

"That is your best tone. It is perfectly formed. Sing it!"

Marian did.

"Now hum it. Hear it inside your head."

Marian did that.

"Now! Come up the scale a note. Hum! . . . Hear it in your head. Sing the same as your E flat! . . . Good! Now make the tone! . . . Sing!"

All this was not as easy as it sounded. But by concentrating she could do it. At least, she could do it on many of the notes of the scale. There were some that her voice would not produce exactly as she heard them in her head when she hummed.

"I will give you exercises that will help with those," Mr. Boghetti said. "Now! Can you breathe?"

Mrs. Patterson had told Marian that her natural way of breathing was excellent for singing. But Mr. Boghetti was not satisfied. Nature could always be improved on.

"Hold your hands hard against your ribs. On the sides, like this! Now! Breathe and see how far you can push apart the hands."

Marian tried, and tried again. She was beginning to see that by exercising the muscles that expanded and contracted her rib cage, she could get greater expansion, which meant more breath to use, and therefore more vocal power.

"You will forget all these things when you are ready to sing," Mr. Boghetti said. "But you must learn before you can afford to forget. You must know *how* and *why!* How you sing, and why it must be that way and no other."

He fixed her with such a stern eye that she felt as if he were trying to hypnotize her into believing him:

"Otherwise—if you sing only by inspiration—one day it will fail you. You will go to the concert hall, and you will not feel like singing. No inspiration! But there is still the audience. The piano begins. They are waiting for you to make the first note.

"That is when you call on what you *know!* That is what makes a professional. That is what I will teach you!"

Chapter *10*

Wrong Turn

H er first years out of high school were wonderful years for Marian, years when everything seemed possible, and many dreams did come true.

She was learning more even than she had hoped to in her work with Mr. Boghetti: things about her voice that gave her a new sort of confidence; things about music that gave her new pleasures and new ambitions. He taught her some of the songs she had heard Roland Hayes sing: Italian arias, French chansons, and even some of the German lieder, which as she learned now, were considered the test of a concert singer's mettle.

She had plenty of chance to put all this new knowledge to work, for she was a real concert singer now, with a manager and an accompanist. At first these two posts were held by different people, but before very long one man did both jobs—the man who for many years was to be her musical partner, Billy King.

Billy was not much older than Marian, but he was established in musical circles in Philadelphia a good while before she was. As choirmaster and organist of an Episcopal church in the city, he had wide contacts. He played for almost all visiting soloists. He had played for Roland Hayes, not only in Philadelphia, but on tour.

It was Mrs. Patterson who first suggested that Billy would be a good person to accompany her, but Marian would never have had the courage to ask him, if he had not volunteered.

It happened one evening when Marian was singing a program at the Y.W.C.A. She had played the accompaniment for her first song, and when she looked up from it, he was standing beside the piano.

"May I?" he asked with a pleasant smile.

It occurred to Marian that he was offering to play because he couldn't bear to hear her do it so badly. But she didn't care. She had no vanity about her ability as a pianist. She was thrilled to have a real one take her place at the keyboard.

Billy was a fine musician. He could have been a great one if he had been willing to work as hard at the piano as Marian did with her voice. But he had a different temperament and a different set of work habits. Things came more easily to him, and the circumstances of his life had been more comfortable. He had never learned to make the sort of hard, sustained effort Marian knew she must make if she was to achieve anything. Billy was more easily distracted

[97]

by temptations to do pleasanter things than practice. So, though he started well ahead of Marian, she caught up and passed him.

But that was later on.

When they first teamed up together, it was Billy who got them most of their engagements, especially those at any distance from Philadelphia.

He tried writing letters to places where he had appeared with Roland Hayes, offering himself and Marian at a modest fee. Surprisingly often, there was a prompt reply.

They played and sang in all sorts of places: churches, clubs, theatres, even private homes. After a year or so, it began to be possible to organize the separate engagements into a regular tour. They travelled as far west as the Mississippi, and as far north as Massachusetts, but the heart of their tours was a group of Negro schools and colleges in the Deep South. Some of them were large and well-known, like Hampton Institute in Virginia, where the composer, Nathaniel Dett, was in charge of the music program and the world-famous choir. Some were even bigger, like Howard University in Washington, or the colleges and schools that combined to make up Atlanta University in Georgia. Others were small backwoods schools in communities that had no movies, and in those days of course no television. There a concert by Billy and Marian was the climax of the year.

For these places Billy and Marian dropped their fee to the barest minimum, but from the others they were soon asking and getting as much as $100 a concert!

Marian could hardly get used to the idea that the years of poverty were over for good. She spent like a sailor, and saved like a miser, by turns. There were so many things she had got used to going without, things she really needed.

Clothes, for instance, had been a problem ever since she began singing in public. Once, when the Andersons were at their poorest, the congregation at Union Baptist took up a collection of $17.02. It was given to Mrs. Anderson to spend on whatever "our Marian" needed most.

What she needed most was shoes; what she wanted most was a dress to wear when she sang. They went down to Wanamaker's, she and her mother, but the cheapest dress that was at all suitable cost $14.98. There wouldn't be enough money left over for shoes.

Mrs. Anderson bought material instead: white satin, and for trimming some narrow gold braid with tiny rosebuds caught in it. With her help, Marian cut out and sewed a dress that looked almost as pretty as the one she couldn't afford.

Under the prodding of necessity, she became quite a good seamstress. She could not only make her own dresses, but alter and fit clothes that were given her. Mrs. Patterson once gave her a real evening gown, which Marian made over for herself and wore in recitals for years, after the white satin had at last worn out.

But now she had less time for dressmaking and more need of dresses. Her platform appearance was very important, especially in the South. Negro audiences, even in cities like Atlanta, were made up for the most part of poor people with high aspirations. They took as much pride in seeing one of their own beautifully and tastefully dressed, as they did in hearing the beauty of her voice. Marian understood this and chose her concert costumes with great care.

They had to be simple, so they would not go out of style. They had to be made of good material, so they would hold up under long use. They had to be flattering to her tall figure and the particular brown of her skin. And they had to be gala—made of fabrics associated with gay or impressive occasions: velvets, satins, laces, or brocades that gleamed with silver or gold.

To be able to buy yards and yards of such fabrics, to be able to hire a dressmaker to help her, or to go to a good store and look through their "better dress" departments without worrying about the price tag—that was a small, but very important dream come true.

There were others that mattered more. One was the possibility of buying or renting a home of their own.

Mrs. Anderson and the three girls had lived on the whole very happily in the big household dominated by Grandmother Anderson. But it had never been the same as the old days when they lived in their own house, run in their own way. They had never stopped hoping to live that way again.

Now it seemed that the time had come. Right across narrow little South Martin Street a small house became vacant. It was the right size and not too expensive.

If it had been any distance away, it would have been hard to reconcile Grandmother Anderson to the move. She was shocked and upset as it was. But finally she was persuaded that the other side of the street was not the other side of the world. Both families could run back and forth to visit at a moment's notice. Besides, their joy and excitement was so contagious that not only the old lady but the entire neighborhood was drawn into it.

The day they moved was a community celebration. Everyone stopped in to admire the improvements that had been made: the new paint, the new draperies, every new piece of furniture. And that greatest improvement of all— Marian's studio!

It was just a tiny room at the back of the second floor, and had once been a bathroom. Marian felt self-conscious about practicing there for fear of disturbing the neighbors on either side. But there was room for her piano and her music and a comfortable chair. She could study, or read, or just be alone. (There was a time coming when a place to be alone was the most valuable possession she had.)

There was one more achievement of those wonderful years, more important than any other. Now at last Marian was able to relieve her mother of the necessity of going out to work.

It was good to be able to do it then. A year or so before, it might have been hard to convince Mrs. Anderson that it was not burdening Marian too much. But at this time she had no choice. She had a sudden illness, serious enough to warn her that she was going to have to change her ways. Even when she was well again, she must not overtax herself.

So she kept busy around her house, doing things she hadn't had time to do for many years, serving her children in other ways, now that she didn't have to be breadwinner as well as homemaker. The girls thrived on the new regime. They loved coming home from school, or work, or engagements to a wonderful, mother-cooked meal in a beautifully kept home. Everyone was happier with the new arrangement, Marian most of all.

Perhaps she was a little too happy, or a little too proud of her own part in providing all this happiness. Perhaps, as her grandmother might have put it, it "went to her head." For it was not long after this, that she decided she was ready to take the giant step she had been dreaming of ever since she began to study with Mr. Boghetti.

"In two years you will be ready to sing anywhere!" he had said when she began.

It was more than two years. She had sung and been well received in Philadelphia's Academy of Music. She had sung several times in New York, the last time to a sold-out house in Harlem. The young impresario who had sponsored that concert said to her, "I think you ought to have a regular downtown musical debut. I would like to have the honor of presenting you at Town Hall!"

Town Hall meant that the concert would be reviewed by New York newspaper and magazine critics. It was the real test of a new performer. Those who passed with flying colors—that is, with good reviews—had arrived. They entered the charmed circle of top-rank concert artists, commanded high fees, appeared on distinguished concert series from coast-to-coast, and in the biggest and best auditoriums everywhere. Those who failed had to content themselves with lower fees, smaller audiences, and a status tactfully described as "recital artist."

Marian felt she had been a recital artist long enough. She was ready for the ordeal that must be undergone to reach the next rank. No one—not even her stern and exacting teacher—warned her that perhaps she was not.

If Mr. Boghetti had any doubts, he kept them to himself. Indeed, he seemed to be enthusiastic about the plan. He helped Marian learn some new Brahms lieder. He gave her all sorts of advice about preparing for the big event, even detailed instructions on how to live every moment of the last few hours: what to eat and when, what time to arrive at the hall, how to warm up and for how long.

Marian followed all his advice to the letter. She and Billy King came up from Philadelphia in the forenoon. Since there was no hotel in midtown New York that would admit her, she took a room at the Y.W.C.A. in Harlem, way uptown. She rested for an hour or so, ate a good supper at four o'clock, met Billy backstage at seven, prepared to do an hour of vocal exercises.

There was no one in the audience yet, of course, but the impresario was there and told them that the ticket sale had been going well. He seemed perfectly confident.

Marian was confident, too. Although she was barely out of her teens—young for a concert debut—she was already a veteran performer. There was nothing really different about tonight from any of the hundreds of nights she and Billy had performed in the last few years. If anything it ought to be easier to sing here than in some of the places they had been on their travels. She was doing quite a few new songs, but even that did not bother her. She had worked hard and Mr. Boghetti seemed satisfied.

At eight o'clock the warm-up was over. Marian and Billy went into the artists' room to relax and wait for their call. They asked how the crowd was and were told that "the hall was filling up nicely."

The concert was advertised for eight-thirty.

They were ready, but eight-thirty came and went, and there was no call. Minutes passed. Eight-forty. Eight-fifty.

They looked at the wall clock every other minute and tried not to look at each other. Was this customary? Did Town Hall audiences come late? Or had something gone wrong? Where was the impresario? Why didn't he come back to report on the attendance and to wish them well?

It was a minute before nine when someone whom they had not seen before appeared and said that they "might as well begin."

The tone was not encouraging, but Marian was still confident as she walked out on stage to bow to her audience.

She stared out into a hall that seemed as empty as the stage on which she stood. Nothing like this had ever happened to her. It took her completely by surprise. A nightmarish sense of loneliness gripped her. She turned to Billy for reassurance.

That was the second shock.

He was not at the piano. She was alone, facing a scattering of strangers.

It was only an instant before she recovered herself and remembered that Billy was accompanying her first song on the organ. The keyboard was way over to one side, almost in the audience. She looked over and there he was, smiling and nodding that he was ready to begin.

She nodded back and closed her eyes. The notes of the organ came from what seemed miles away. She was remembering Mr. Boghetti's warning about the moment when inspiration would fail her. It had come. She would have to depend on what she had learned from him—the how and the why.

She managed to get through the opening song without a false note or a quaver, but the effort was enormous. Each tone seemed to have to lift a heavy stone before it could make its way out. There was no joy in the singing.

After that it was easier because Billy was at the piano giving her moral support. But the new songs made problems for her. She regretted bitterly that she had chosen them. It was because Roland Hayes had sung them at his Town Hall debut and she wanted to prove to herself that she could do what he had done. But she couldn't.

It wasn't only the difficulty of the music. It was something she had never felt before about singing the German lyrics. She knew in a general way what they meant, but she had learned them sound for sound, not word for word. She wasn't always sure where one word ended and the next began. It seemed to her tonight that she had been caught in a lie.

There wasn't time to analyze this strange shamed feeling. The concert was off to a bad start, but it had to go on.

The applause when she finished, sounded halfhearted to Marian. Her own heart was like lead. For the first time in her whole life, she felt that she had failed.

She lay awake in the little room at the Y until late in the night, thinking about everything that had gone wrong, especially the Brahms. It seemed to her now that the feeling of deceit came from having pretended to be something she was not: the mistress of many languages. But perhaps there was more to it. For singing was, after all, a way of speaking. How could she speak what she didn't understand herself?

One of the critics whose review she read next morning, put it even more plainly.

"She sang her Brahms as if by rote."

By rote! Like a parrot!

It was cruelly, crushingly true.

Billy tried to make excuses for her by blaming those who had kept back the truth about the empty house till it was too late for her to adjust to the shock. But if she had been the professional she thought herself, she could have given her best performance under any condition.

She remembered the story of the night Roland Hayes sang in London, almost delirious with fever, fighting for his life against pneumonia, but so beautifully that he was commanded to sing the whole program again for the King and Queen. It was the turning point of his career.

This night might be the turning point of hers, but if so, it was a turn in the wrong direction. She would never have another such chance. She didn't deserve one.

She would never sing in public again. She couldn't bear to. She didn't think she could bear to sing at all.

Chapter 11

Comeback

Marian's mother and sisters did their best to make it easy for her. They said nothing about the concert. They went through the routines of daily living as if nothing had happened, as if there were nothing odd in the silence where there had been music. They asked no questions about what Marian did during those long hours she spent in her studio. They gave her what she needed most, time for the wounds in her pride to heal.

The wounds healed faster because of one other thing her family did for her without meaning to. Her love for them drove her back to her music sooner than she might otherwise have gone. For music was many things to Marian, and one of them was a way of earning money.

No one had to tell her that if her mother was to stay on at home, if the payments on the house were to be kept up, Marian must go on earning money in sizable amounts. Singing was the only way she knew to do that.

As soon as she could bear to open her piano and strike a note, she began to do vocal exercises. After a few weeks, she called Mr. Boghetti and asked if she could come for a lesson.

He said yes and named a time.

Brusque and easily irritated—with plenty of irritating habits of his own—Mr. Boghetti could be wonderfully tactful when he wanted to be. Better even than her family, he understood what Marian was going through, and that she had to get through it by herself.

He showed his sympathy by his silence. In the old days he would have insisted that she come for her lesson at a regular hour on a regular day of the week, so that he could schedule other pupils before and after her. Now he let her come when she felt like it, or stay away without explanation or excuse. He never referred to the disastrous concert or gave his opinion of what had gone wrong.

Finally Marian found the courage to ask his advice about one thing.

"I must do something about my languages," she said. "I remember once when I sang at the University of Pennsylvania, a young man went to all the trouble to look up my address in the phone book and come round one Sunday afternoon to tell me that anyone who sang as well as I did ought to be ashamed to pronounce the words of foreign songs so badly."

Was there something Mr. Boghetti could suggest about her French and her Italian, and most of all, her German?

[*108*]

French and Italian, yes. Mr. Boghetti had a pupil who could help her improve her French accent. He himself would be glad to help with her Italian. But for German he had no solution.

"Except to give up the lieder."

He was not serious. He knew how much they meant to Marian, how much she loved them, and how important they were in any singer's repertory.

But Billy King made almost the same suggestion quite seriously.

"Give them up till you can go to Germany and learn to speak the language. That's the quickest way in the long run."

Meanwhile they could plan a set of acceptable programs without the Brahms. And it was time they started planning programs, he reminded her. The dates for their next concert season had been booked months before. Marian had feared that the bad New York notices might cause some cancellations, but there had been none so far. The usual publicity mailing had actually brought in a few new dates.

Marian spent a couple of afternoons with Billy, going over their old programs and thinking of ways to improve them. All at once she realized that she was back in the groove.

But back in the groove was back in a rut, as far as advancing herself was concerned.

Her failure had not killed her ambition. She still felt that her voice was meant to be used for greater things than

[109]

she had yet done. She had learned humility and caution, but she had not learned to settle for less than the best.

Mr. Boghetti sensed her impatience and finally he made a suggestion: that she enter a voice contest in Philadelphia. It was under the auspices of the Philharmonic Society so it had prestige, although there would not be many contestants and the prize was not large.

Marian decided to try.

She worked on some new songs, worked harder than usual, trying to keep herself from thinking of the moment when she would have to stand and sing before judges . . . whether at such a moment she would be drained of confidence as she had been on the stage at Town Hall. . . .

The only way to find out was to take the risk of another failure.

She worked hard, and Mr. Boghetti worked hard. Sometimes he would move away from the piano to listen to her, arms folded, forehead wrinkled into a terrible frown, his eye fixed on her in that hypnotic stare. It was like a preview of the contest, and Marian felt a little surer of herself each time she managed to sing in spite of him.

When the moment finally came and she stood before the judges, she looked over at the front row of spectators' seats, and there was Mr. Boghetti, arms folded, forehead wrinkled, eye fixed. She could feel that eye on her even when she closed hers. He was forcing her to do what he wanted—and what she wanted.

It worked. She sang at her best. And she won.

It was the first time the prize had gone to a Negro singer, and the papers made much of that. But after a week or so, Marian realized that there would be no new requests for concerts as a result.

What the contest did accomplish was to give her back her confidence. Mr. Boghetti lost no time testing it.

"Why not the Lewisohn Stadium Contest now?"

That was a real challenge. There would be hundreds of contestants from all over the country, two sets of preliminary rounds before the finals. Marian would be competing against the best young voices in America, and in New York —the city where she had failed. The prize was an appearance with the New York Philharmonic Orchestra in one of its outdoor concerts at Lewisohn Stadium!

Marian said she would try.

Each contestant had to prepare an operatic aria and two other songs. Mr. Boghetti selected an aria by an Italian composer, Donizetti, and two songs in English.

They went to work.

They worked through June and into July. It was one of Philadelphia's muggy summers when the city felt like a steam room. Marian needed a way to cool off, so she signed up for another set of lessons—the swimming course at the Y.W.C.A. She had always meant to do something about the fact that she couldn't swim a stroke, and this seemed a fine time.

She went regularly to the classes, but the results were not encouraging. Marian was not a natural swimmer. In fact she was a nonswimmer. All her hard work got her nothing but an occasional noseful of pool water. Her ears began to bother her. She plugged them with cotton and floundered on, determined to see the course through to the end whether she ever learned to swim or not.

But in spite of her determination, she had to miss one of the last classes because it fell on the day of the elimination round of the contest.

Every one of the contestants—and there were 300 of them—had an accompanist, and most had a teacher with them too. The crowd filled the whole ground floor of Aeolian Hall.

At the appointed hour, the rules were announced over a public address system from the balcony, where the judges sat—heard but not seen. They explained that there was not time for each contestant to sing all the material he or she had prepared. The judges would listen to what they felt to be a fair sample. Then a clicker would sound. The singer was to stop and leave the stage.

"Pay no attention," Mr. Boghetti whispered in Marian's ear. "If they stop you, pretend you don't hear. Go on to the end. Be sure you get in that final trill."

"Go on singing when they tell me to stop?"

Marian was appalled at such boldness, but Mr. Boghetti believed in boldness.

"Not for everybody, maybe. But for you. You must insist that they hear you out."

Marian said nothing, but she didn't believe she could do what he was asking. Hard as it was to disobey her teacher, it would be harder to disobey the unseen judges.

Meanwhile she had drawn a number and was waiting her turn. By the time it came near, several other singers had sung her Donizetti aria. Not one of them had got to the final trill. Each time the clicker cut short their song, Marian winced. Each time she winced, Mr. Boghetti glared a warning at her.

"What if I skip the recitative and start with the aria itself?" she whispered.

He shook his head. "Sing it all. Make them listen!"

The next contestants got only a minute or two apiece. It was her turn.

She began with the half-spoken recitative, though it seemed a waste of precious time. She could feel her teacher's hypnotic eye on her, reminding her of his command. She was expecting at any instant the sound of the clicker and the awful decision—which command to disobey?

But the clicker didn't sound.

Maybe she didn't hear it. (Her ears had felt a little dull since her last ducking in the Y pool.) She was well into the aria now! Singing as if each note might be the last—as indeed it might! On and on to the great final trill! She sang it through to the last beautiful flourish!

There was a second of dead silence. Then applause broke out all over Aeolian Hall.

An angry voice on the loud speaker reminded the audience that applause was forbidden. Then it asked Marian whether she had another song.

She sang one of her English songs, and went back to her seat.

"Did the clicker sound?" she asked Mr. Boghetti.

"No! You are the only who who has finished the aria! Not to speak of a second song!"

They left soon afterwards to catch the train back to Philadelphia. Mr. Boghetti was elated by her success, but as always he found things that could be improved. He talked about them all the way home, which gave Marian a chance to relax and become aware of something very peculiar about one of her ears.

It was not so much pain as a sort of numbness. She said nothing about it. She had never mentioned the swimming lessons to Mr. Boghetti and she suspected that he was not going to approve. Not if the trouble in her ear had anything to do with them.

Perhaps it would be better to give up swimming.

Two days later Mr. Boghetti called her on the phone. "You have won!"

"Won?"

"You are one of 16 who will sing in the semifinals. Four will be chosen from them."

So it was back to work in the muggy heat. Marian was almost tempted to go back to the Y pool, just to cool off a little, but her ear still felt strange. She thought once of going to a doctor, but it got no worse, and she really had no time to spare.

On the second trip to New York, Mr. Boghetti was full of ambitious hopes. He was talking about how he would coach Marian for the Lewisohn Stadium appearance, assuming that she would win today's round, and go on to win the finals. Marian wished she could share his enthusiasm, but she felt wooden beside him.

In fact, she felt worse than wooden. Her ear was beginning to hurt.

She had thought when she got up this morning that there was something stuck in it. Perhaps it was one of the little cotton plugs she had used to keep the water out while she swam. She tried pulling it out, first with her fingers, then with tweezers, but working at it made it worse.

By the time they got to Aeolian Hall, she had a real old-fashioned earache. Not unbearable yet, but getting worse.

"It won't be so long today," Mr. Boghetti said cheerfully. "There are only 16 contestants. You may be one of the first."

Marian hoped so. She was not sure how long she could hold out. But Mr. Boghetti was right; she was called after only a half hour's wait.

She had to sing her aria and both her other songs. As soon as she was through, Mr. Boghetti took her back to his studio to rest until train time.

"Why do you look so discouraged?" he asked. "You did well. Very well!"

Marian was tempted to tell him that it was not discouragement he saw on her face. But it had got too bad to talk about at all. She felt as if there were some horrible growth deep inside her ear. Her hearing was affected. What if it turned out to be permanent? Beethoven had gone deaf, and he had gone on composing and conducting, but who ever heard of a deaf singer?

The phone rang and Mr. Boghetti answered it.

"What? . . . Are you sure? . . . All right, all right!"

He turned back to Marian with a dazed look, which could be the shock of joy or the shock of defeat.

[*115*]

"There are to be no finals," he said. "It is unanimous. You will sing on August 25th at Lewisohn Stadium!"

At that moment Marian was wondering whether she would ever sing anywhere again.

But the growth in her ear was only an abcess. As soon as it was lanced and the pressure relieved, the pain began to ease.

"Will I be deaf?" she asked her doctor.

"Not if you take care of yourself, and stay out of swimming pools for the rest of the summer."

Orders she didn't mind obeying for the rest of that summer and several summers to come!

Chapter *12*

Crest of the Wave

The Lewisohn Stadium Concert was the high point of Marian's life till that moment, both in itself and in what it promised for the future.

A trainload of family and friends and loyal Philadelphians came up to see "their Marian" sing with the whole of a great symphony orchestra to accompany her. It was a beautiful warm evening. The Stadium was full of people dressed in their summer best. Marian, too, had a new dress, elegant and flattering.

She bought it at Wanamaker's—the same store where she had once had to pass up a dress that cost $14.98. The new dress of lovely pale blue crepe was more than just a dress. It measured something: how far she had come, how far she hoped still to go.

Marian had rehearsed with the orchestra and conductor and she was not nervous. But it was a tremendous thrill to walk the narrow aisle between music stands and take her place just to the right of conductor Willem Van Hoogstraten's little box-like podium; to receive not only the applause of the audience's hands but also the quiet little taps of violin bows against music stands that was the musicians' applause.

She had atoned for the failure at Town Hall. There were good reviews this time, not only in New York papers, but nationally, for the Lewisohn Stadium Contest was a national affair. There ought to be new opportunities for her and Billy. There were.

Requests began to come in from places as far west as California, as far north as Canada. For the first time well-known concert series managers made inquiries about her schedule. There was an invitation to sing with the Hampton Institute Choir at Carnegie Hall.

It was not the same as giving a concert there on her own, but it was a step up. Marian sang "Listen to the Lambs," which was composed by Nathaniel Dett, leader of the Hampton Choir. She loved the song and she sang it well. Before the rest of the program was over, a man came backstage to see her—Mr. Arthur Judson, of the Judson Concert Bureau.

This was one of the most respected managements in the business. Mr. Judson was offering his own services as her manager and talking about fees of $750 per concert! (*"Mark my words, Mrs. Anderson, one day that child is going to be earning as much as $50 a night!"*) He would guarantee that she appeared on all the important concert series, in all the major cities of America. Would she be interested?

[*118*]

Marian tried not to sound too interested, and said yes. They made a date to meet and work out details of a contract at his Philadelphia office.

She felt as if her long effort had been finally rewarded, as if now a great wave lifted her over the last barrier, into the magic land about which she had dreamed since the day she had tried to enroll in the conservatory.

It was a lovely feeling while it lasted, but it did not last out the week.

When she went to keep her appointment at the Philadelphia office, she found Mr. Judson changed. He spoke now of a fee of $500. It was not only less money; it placed her in a category of clients whose affairs he did not handle personally. Someone else on his staff would do it, do the very best that could be done for her, he said. She and Billy were to hand over the card file they kept of all the places they had appeared or been invited to appear. Future inquiries were to be referred to the Judson office, which would get out a special publicity folder. For this and any other expenses the office was put to she was to pay, plus, of course, the usual percentage of every fee she earned.

Mr. Judson made no explanation of the difference between this proposal and the one he had made in New York. Marian could only guess what might have happened in those few days. Had someone told him about her Town Hall fiasco? Had he read those old bad reviews? Or had he realized, when he stopped to think about it, that a Negro singer presented special problems to a manager, that there were many places where she would not be welcome at $750 or at any other fee?

[119]

(Years later someone suggested to her that the real reason was quite different. Mr. Judson had at that time another client, also a contralto, a very famous and very temperamental lady, who might have been jealous of sharing her personal manager with a rival like Marian.)

Marian had her doubts about signing a contract on these new terms. She and Billy King could get $500 in some places without having to pay for special publicity. On the other hand, the new arrangement would relieve them of thousands of time-consuming business details. Marian longed to be free to concentrate on her music and leave business to someone else. Perhaps it was worth a try for that advantage alone.

She decided to sign and see what happened. If things went well the first season, maybe better terms could be worked out for the second.

What happened was nothing. No change, either for the better or for the worse.

Marian and Billy appeared only at places they had sung before; the special publicity folder brought no new engagements. Actually there were fewer, because places that couldn't afford the new fee were dropped from the schedule. Those that had paid $500 before did so again, and a few places raised their fee to meet the new price.

But when it was all added up at the end of the season, Marian had made the same income by singing fewer concerts.

The second season was a little better. The Judson office publicity brought in a few new dates. But no new terms were proposed. The fee was still $500. Marian was still not important enough for Mr. Judson's personal attention.

It seemed that the great wave that had lifted her so high was letting her down, very gently, at the same place on the beach. Or, to put it less pleasantly, she was back in the same old rut.

Marian did a lot of thinking about the reasons, but she reached no real understanding. Sometimes she wondered if her ambition was deceiving her. Maybe she had risen as far as she had any musical right to rise. Yet she couldn't believe that, even in her moments of deepest discouragement.

She kept trying new things. Once, for instance, she decided to go to another teacher, a move that hurt Mr. Boghetti's feelings so that he refused to continue giving her lessons so long as she was going to the other man. Marian learned new things from the new coach, but nothing that made any difference to her career.

Finally she went to talk to Mr. Judson, to ask if he had any plans or suggestions to make, and to try out on him a plan that had been taking shape very slowly in her own mind.

"As a matter of fact I've been talking about you a good deal lately," he said, "with a friend of mine who knows more about voice than most people in the concert business. She tells me she suspects you may really be a soprano. How would you like to spend an hour with her? Let her test your voice and decide what your range really is."

Decide whether she was a soprano or a contralto? Decide whether she had been singing all these years in the wrong register? Marian was too shocked to be angry. If her manager had no confidence that she was on the right track in something as fundamental as this, it was no wonder he had been able to do so little for her.

"I know perfectly well I'm not a soprano," she said. "Do you think perhaps I ought to go to Europe?"

"What in the world for?"

There were many reasons, some of which ought to have been obvious to Mr. Judson. For one thing, Marian wanted to learn foreign languages and that was the best way. For another, she wanted to learn some of the finer points of lieder singing for which no American teacher could be found.

Also it was no secret that many Negro artists had not been able to break the barriers raised against them in their own country until they had gone abroad and won fame there. It was well-known that there was far less prejudice in Europe, and it was still true that Americans looked to the Old World for guidance in many fields of art, especially in music. (Opera singers with good American names changed them to Italian-sounding ones to make their way easier at home, not in Italy!)

But the most urgent reason was the desperation Marian felt as she went round and round in the circle from which Mr. Judson had once promised to release her.

"If you go to Europe, it will be to satisfy your own vanity," he said disapprovingly.

That meant to her that he didn't believe she would make good, wouldn't reach the top, anywhere, under any circumstances!

If that was the state of affairs, it was just as well to know it, Marian thought to herself.

"All right," she said aloud. "Let it be for that."

Chapter 13

"I Have Not Yet Crowned You"

The big decision was made, but there were dozens of smaller ones to make, each important in its own way.

Could she afford the trip this year, or must she wait till she had saved more money ahead? How much would it cost? How long could she plan to stay? What about her mother and sisters?

Her sisters urged her to go. They could look after their mother without her now. There was money in the bank, and they were working. Her mother was eager for Marian to give herself every advantage she needed. She would miss her, but she had her other children to keep her busy. Billy King, who had lived abroad, helped Marian work out a budget of probable expenses. Little by little, she was coming to see that the trip was possible at the end of this season!

Where should she go?

She decided—after much consultation—on England. It would be easier to make the adjustment to living away from her own country for the first time if she didn't have to adjust to a new language too. Also, Roland Hayes had gone first to England, and Marian found it reassuring to be following a trail he had opened. Finally, it turned out that one of the greatest teachers of lieder singing, Master Raimund von Zur Mühlen, was living there.

Lawrence Brown, who had been Roland Hayes' accompanist in England, was willing to write to Master von Zur Mühlen and recommend Marian as a pupil. The answer came back: the Master was not taking many pupils, but he would listen to Miss Anderson.

"If he does take you on, you will learn more about singing Brahms—as well as Schubert and Schumann and Beethoven—than you could learn from any teacher in Germany today," Lawrence Brown told her.

As the season drew toward a close, decisions crowded thicker and faster. What ship should she sail on? What clothes should she pack? What music should she take with her? How much money should she carry and in what form?

Billy King was almost as excited as she. Every day he had a new idea. One of them was to write his friend, Roger Quilter, a wealthy British patron of the arts.

Mr. Quilter wrote back to say he would be delighted to be of any assistance to Miss Anderson. He could get up a list of possible places for her to live—something Marian needed, for she couldn't afford to stay in a hotel any length of time. Would Miss Anderson be good enough to phone him as soon as she arrived in London?

[124]

Marian tucked Mr. Quilter's phone number into her purse along with a dozen other important phone numbers and addresses and papers: her passport, her letter of credit to a British bank, her packet of traveler's checks, and the letter of introduction to Master von Zur Mühlen. Finally she added to the collection a steamship ticket on the great French ocean liner, the *Ile de France*.

She was really going. She could believe it at last.

Marian enjoyed every moment of the crossing, although it was a little lonely.

The passengers were mostly white Americans who did not make friendly overtures. But her concert tours had taught her to find substitutes for human companionship when it was not offered. She began trying out her high-school French on the stewards and stewardesses. She went over all the music in her music case, studying it as she had long promised herself she was going to as soon as she had the time.

She had almost got used to the sensation of having nothing really pressing to do—and enjoying it—when she was told that the ship would let passengers off at Southampton next day. It was time to start packing all over again.

She went over everything very carefully, making sure all the papers she would need were where she could get at them easily. She must have her passport for immigration, the list of what was in her luggage to show at customs inspection, her ticket on the boat train from Southampton to London, enough money to change into pounds, shilling, and pence, so that she could tip porters, pay for taxis, and make telephone calls.

Her purse was too full. Every time she opened it, she had to struggle to get it closed again; so she decided to remove everything nonessential. Things like traveler's checks and her letter of credit—all the papers she would not need till later—she put into her music case which could be locked and which she would carry with her. The rest of her luggage was to be checked through to the Paddington Station in London.

Congratulating herself on her foresight and thoroughness, Marian went up on deck to watch the ship come in to port and to get her first glimpse of a foreign country.

England looked very much like America.

Once she got on land, she found a few differences. Automobiles and buses ran on the wrong side of the streets, trains on the wrong side of the tracks. English trains were different in other ways, too, cut up into compartments seating six passengers, each with a door leading directly to the platform, as well as to the aisle. People spoke in a collection of different accents, some of which were hard for her to understand at first.

On the whole, however, Marian felt a little letdown, but very much at home.

Everything went very smoothly at the immigration and customs offices, and in no time at all, she was on the last leg of her journey, speeding along toward London, thinking how good it was to know that somewhere in the great city that would be in darkness when she reached it, there was one person at least who was expecting her.

"Where to?" asked the porter who helped her find her luggage in the station.

"I don't know yet. I have to make a phone call to find out where I am to stay."

Marian asked the porter to wait while she found a booth and dropped a sixpence into the slot.

"Yes?" A very cultivated male voice came on the line.

"Mr. Quilter, this is Marian Anderson. I've just arrived."

There was a pause.

"Who did you say?" The voice was very cool indeed.

"Marian Anderson."

Again the odd, unfriendly pause.

Flustered and a little hurt, Marian spelled out her name and then thought to ask, "This *is* Mr. Quilter, isn't it?"

"No, madam."

"Oh!" she gasped. "Do I have the wrong number? I'm calling Mr. Quilter's house. Mr. Roger Quilter—"

"Yes, madam."

Whoever owned this superrefined voice was not giving away any information! It was like a guessing game in which you had to think of the right question.

"Is Mr. Roger Quilter at home?" she asked.

"No, madam. He is in a nursing home."

It took a second or two for her to translate the unfamiliar "nursing home" into "hospital." Then she understood everything.

Mr. Quilter had been taken suddenly ill. He forgot to leave any word with his servant. It was not really his fault, since he had no definite idea of when she would be

[127]

coming. It was certainly not the fault of his very correct manservant. All the same, a stranger in a strange city, with a cart full of luggage, and no place to stay the night! And a porter impatiently waiting for her to pay him off so he could look for another job!

After a moment in which her mind was a perfect, frightening blank, she remembered that there were other phone numbers in her book, which she had fortunately put into her purse. There was John Payne, a Negro actor who now made his home in England. He had visited the Andersons on his last trip home and urged Marian to come to England.

"Be sure to call us when you do," he said. "My wife and I would like to have you stay with us."

Marian looked for his phone number, murmuring a little prayer that the Paynes would be in their own—not a nursing—home. She dropped another sixpence into the phone and held her breath.

Mrs. Payne answered. She recognized Marian's name and sounded delighted that she was calling. Of course she must come and stay with them! There was plenty of room. Here were the directions to give the cabby.

Feeling wonderfully lighthearted, Marian left the booth, called the porter and let him bundle her and all her baggage into one of those great roomy London cabs. Not till after she had been welcomed and warmed at the Paynes' living-room grate fire, did she suddenly realize she was also light-handed.

She had lost her music case. The case into which she had carefully locked all her most precious papers, including her money! Whether she had left it in the phone booth, or on the boat train, or just dropped it somewhere as she fumbled for something in her purse, she had no idea. But she was almost ill with distress.

The Paynes tried to calm her. Traveler's checks can be cancelled if lost, and new ones issued. That's why one carries them instead of cash. A letter of credit can't be used by anyone without proper identification. If she didn't find it in a day or so, she could write back to her bank in Philadelphia, and they would send a new one. The lost letters of introduction could all be duplicated, and even the lost music was replaceable.

"But the chances are you won't have to do any of this," John Payne said. "You'll find the case in the morning. In the lost-and-found at the station or the cab company."

"And if not, you can always go to Scotland Yard," said Mrs. Payne.

Marian went to bed and tried to sleep, but her first night in England was not a restful one. When she did drop off, her dreams were full of Sherlock Holmes giving Dr. Watson his poor opinion of the efficiency of Scotland Yard.

The Paynes turned out to be right. Marian found the lost case in the last place she looked for it (short of Scotland Yard): the lost-and-found in Paddington Station. She had left it in the phone booth where she made the call.

By the time she got back from this adventure, the Paynes had called Mr. Quilter's home and found out that he was over the crisis of his illness and on the mend. He sent a message that he was anxious to make good on his offers of assistance to Marian just as soon as he was permitted visitors.

She had been in England less than 24 hours, had two bad scares and two happy endings—enough excitement to last her the rest of her stay.

As soon as she had her letter of introduction safe in her possession again, she mailed it off to Master von Zur Mühlen. A day or so later came an answer saying that he was not well, but he would receive her. Marian made the trip out to the lovely little country town in which he lived and knocked at his door exactly at the appointed hour.

She was ushered into the studio, where the Master sat in a high-backed chair, his knees wrapped in a red rug, one hand resting on the head of a cane, like a king on his throne. Marian was shocked to see how old and how frail he was, for all his regal air of authority.

"Sing," he commanded, when the greetings were done.

She handed her music to a quiet man who had come from somewhere to play the piano. She had chosen one of her Brahms songs, partly as a compliment to the music of Master's homeland, partly because this was what she wished to study with him if he would take her. He let her sing it through to the end.

"Come here!"

Marian walked the length of the room to stand in front of him, feeling like a child who has been summoned to punishment for some mischief, but what, she didn't know.

"Do you know what that song means?"

"I know in general. I don't know it word for—"

"If you don't know, don't sing it!"

She felt punished, but at least she knew why. And she agreed. She had thought something like this herself after the Town Hall concert.

"Sing something you do know," said Master.

Marian began a song in English, an old spiritual that she knew so well it was second nature to her. Instantly she felt the difference, the freedom that full understanding gave her. Her voice began to soar, as it used to in the choir loft when she was too full of the joy of song to hold it in.

" . . . *He's got the little bitsy baby in His hands.*
He's got the whole world in His hands."

There was a terrible banging noise. The piano stopped. Marian stopped, and opened her eyes.

Master was banging on the bare floor with his cane, and smiling at her at the same time.

"You are singing like a queen," he said. "And I have not yet crowned you."

Marian puzzled a good deal over what he meant by that. But she was not left in suspense about the purpose of her visit. Master said at once that he would take her as a pupil. He gave her a Schubert song to work on, and told her to come back the next day to sing it for him.

Very much excited, Marian went back to the village and took a room in a private house where there was a piano she could use. She worked hard on her new song, but just before she was to leave for her lesson the next day, there was a call from Master's house.

He was ill and would not be able to see her after all. She would be called as soon as he could.

By the time the call came, the Schubert was very well prepared indeed. Master listened, nodded approvingly, and gave her a few very interesting suggestions. He seemed much weaker than before, and Marian felt he was taxing himself to give her even the half hour he did. But she got so much out of it that she decided Lawrence Brown was right. This was the one man in the world who could teach her what she wanted to learn about lieder. Lessons with him made the whole journey worthwhile.

She made arrangements to stay on in the village, rented a piano and a larger room, moved her music and most of her clothes out from London, and waited for the summons to her next lesson.

She waited nearly two weeks. When the call came, it was bad news. Master von Zur Mühlen would not be able to give her or anyone else lessons. He had suffered a stroke. His teaching days were done.

Back in London, Marian tried to make the best of what opportunities still offered.

She found a teacher who had studied with Master and knew his way of approaching the lieder. She found another teacher to work with her on special problems of vocal technique: Amanda Ira Aldridge, daughter of a famous American Negro actor who had gone to England to play Othello, and never returned to the States.

Roger Quilter, when she finally met him, was just as cordial as the Paynes and able to be more of help to her than they. Professional musicians and patrons of music gathered regularly at his home for evenings of fine music. He made Marian welcome at these parties, had her sing for his guests, and finally arranged for her to give two public recitals in London. At one of them he accompanied her himself, and she sang some songs of his composition.

It was a pleasant life, as well as a rewarding one, the first time Marian had lived out from under the shadow of Jim Crow. It gave her a sense of freedom she had never known before, which she would always miss a little, now that she had tasted it.

Still, she never thought seriously of doing as the Paynes or Ira Aldridge had done. They were happy with the choice they had made. But Marian could no more imagine changing her nationality than she could imagine changing families.

One was what one was born, for better or worse.

Chapter *14*

Rave Notices

The time passed much too quickly, and all at once she was back in Philadelphia, being interviewed by the publicity man in the Judson office. He was looking for new material to put in the brochure that went out every summer announcing her next winter's tour.

"Did you give any concerts in Europe?"

"Yes," said Marian. "In London."

"At Queen's Hall?"

"No. At Wigmore Hall."

He had never heard of such a place. It was, of course, not as famous or as glamorous as Queen's Hall, but—as Marian explained to him—it was there Roland Hayes gave the concert that led to his command performance before the King and Queen.

"Did you sing for the King and Queen?" he asked, showing interest for the first time.

"No."

The light in his eyes died. "Did you get any reviews?"

Marian had brought home the reviews of her concerts. They were brief and reserved, in the usual British style. The publicity man read them and shook his head.

"Not what we need, I'm afraid."

What he wanted was quotable phrases like "greatest voice of the century!" "Most brilliant concert of the year!" "Sensational!" "Unbelievable!" "Superb!"

Without such praise, her foreign trip was an expensive failure from the publicity point of view. Mr. Judson's gloomy prediction seemed to have justified itself. There wasn't a single new date on her tour, not one place where a higher fee was paid.

Worst of all, she had learned no German. She felt the lack of it every time she sang her lieder and remembered Master von Zur Mühlen saying, "If you don't know, don't sing it."

When someone asked her one day where she would go and what she would study if she had a chance to return to Europe, she answered instantly.

"To Berlin, to learn German."

It happened that the men who asked the question were representatives of the Rosenwald Fund, set up by a great Jewish philanthropist of Chicago, who was interested in improving educational opportunities for Negroes. Marian's need was exactly the sort a Rosenwald fellowship was intended to meet. It was offered to her then and there.

One thing Marian decided before she sailed this time: she would not come home without something to show for her time and money that could be used in a practical, direct way to advance her American career. She would give a concert in the best hall in Berlin, and see to it that the critics of the most influential newspapers and magazines attended and heard the sort of program they would review seriously.

There was only one way to accomplish all this in a city where she had neither reputation nor friends. That was to pay her own expenses.

Most singers did that anyway. Marian hadn't, because at the time of her Town Hall debut she had no money to invest in such a venture, and the impresario had been able and willing to raise the money elsewhere. The fact that he had done so badly—for her, as well as for himself—had taught her the importance of having a good manager, a man of experience and judgment and wide contacts and good taste. She meant to choose her Berlin manager as carefully as she chose her singing teacher.

Getting herself settled was —as she expected—much more complicated than it had been in England, because at first she could neither understand what was said to her nor make herself understood. She found rooms in the home of an actor who spoke a few words of English, and was willing to teach her German. His wife spoke no English at all; so Marian had to learn the German words for everything she needed: food at the table, hot water and soap for the bath, more or less heat in her room. Under this pressure it was amazing how fast she began to speak.

She found a teacher who would help her polish her lieder for the stern test of a performance before German critics. And she found a manager.

He was recommended to her by the Judson office, and he impressed Marian as someone who understood his business and could be relied on to do anything he promised.

The way must be carefully prepared for the sort of Berlin appearance she had in mind, he told her. It ought to be in the famous Bachsaal (named for the great German composer, Johann Sebastian Bach), and the publicity that preceded it must be of a certain quality to make sure that the important Berlin critics would be attracted. He would guarantee to get them there. It was up to Marian to get their praise.

The cost of such a concert—most of which must be paid in advance—was higher than Marian had expected. More than half her Rosenwald grant, which was intended to cover her expenses for six months! However, Marian had saved money of her own for this trip. She could pay for the concert out of that. She might have to go home a little sooner than she had intended. But what was the use of staying longer without achieving her objective?

Marian thought it over for a few days and made up her mind. She handed over to her new manager a good big slice of her savings. Having done it, she gave herself no chance to worry over whether she had made a mistake but went right to work on her German and on her songs.

As she came out of the studio after her voice lesson one day, she found two gentlemen waiting for her. They both rose and bowed.

"May I present myself?" said the older of the two, in excellent English. "My name is Rasmussen. This is my friend, Kosti Vehanen."

Marian Anderson and her teacher, Berlin, 1931

Mr. Rasmussen was a Norwegian impresario looking for new artists to introduce to audiences in his own and the other Scandinavian countries. Vehanen was a pianist look-ing for a singer with whom to work. Would it be possible for them to hear Miss Anderson sing?

Marian took them back into the studio, where her teacher made them welcome. She picked out two of the lieder on which she had just been working and some of her spirituals. Vehanen played for her, and she was as impressed with his musicianship as he was, apparently, with hers.

"Would you be interested in a tour with Vehanen as your accompanist?" Rasmussen asked.

A tour for which she would be paid, instead of having to pay! It was the first such offer she had ever had in Europe. Marian was grateful for the boost it gave her morale, but she didn't want to make any decision till after her Bachsaal concert. She thanked Mr. Rasmussen and promised to give him her answer in a few weeks.

The Bachsaal was well filled when she came out to take her bow. The applause was polite, though a trifle cool. Her manager had carried out his part of the bargain. The rest was up to her.

Her first group was applauded, but not warmly. Her second—all songs by Schubert—got a better response. Her third group, which were songs in English, were still better received. When she came to the spirituals, she got a real ovation.

Marian felt satisfied. She could hardly wait to see if she had satisfied the critics, too.

But she couldn't find a word in any of the newspapers next day. Nor the day after. Nor the day after that. The concert might as well never have taken place.

Marian was appalled and mystified.

What had gone wrong this time? Had she failed so badly that no one was going to bother to say so? Had her manager failed to get the critics there after all? She worried for nearly a week before she asked the actor and his wife.

"It's too soon!" they told her. "Our critics don't rush from the concert hall to their offices as yours in America do. They take time to think; they write and then polish what they have written. You will get reviews. You must be a little patient."

While Marian was being patient, she had a letter from Mr. Rasmussen with definite details about the tour he was proposing. There would be at least three cities, possibly one or two more. She would give a pair of concerts in each. The fee he was offering was not large, but if they were as successful as he hoped, it would be raised. At worst, it would more than pay her expenses for the time she would spend. At best, it would make up some of what she had invested in the Bachsaal venture.

Oslo, Helsinki, Stockholm, Bergen, Stavanger, Copenhagen . . . there was a wonderful strangeness about even the names of those cities of the Far North. Marian knew some of the music of the great Scandinavian composers, but she had never sung it because she didn't feel that she entirely understood it. Traveling in these countries might give her new insight into the roots of their music.

The Berlin reviews began to appear at last. They were all very complimentary. Not quite as extravagant as an American press agent would like, but good enough to prove that Marian had succeeded in one of her objects. She had learned to sing the great music of Germany well enough to please the most discriminating musical taste of that country. And no one had any criticism to make of the way she pronounced the words.

There were only a few weeks left before she must go home, for there were concert dates awaiting her there.

Why not devote the time to a real adventure like the Scandinavian tour?

It proved to be the most significant adventure of her whole life. For Marian was an immediate and enormous —sensational!—success in the northern countries.

Her way was made easier by two things, neither of which had helped her at home: her name and the color of her skin.

"Anderson is a Swedish and a Danish name," Kosti explained. "But most Swedish or Danish Andersons have never seen a Negro. You are a seven-day wonder to them."

He made her understand that there was nothing unfriendly or mocking in this wonder. People were simply fascinated by her. Children followed her on the streets and sometimes shyly touched her, marvelling that anyone so like them in other ways could be so different in coloring.

Kosti advised her to wear clothes that emphasized the difference. Marian needed a second concert gown, since she had brought only one with her and was giving two concerts in every city she visited. When Mrs. Rasmussen took her shopping, she decided to follow Kosti's advice, and chose a gown of chalky white crepe that made her brown skin look even browner by contrast. Sure enough, it and her appearance were mentioned by the critics, who, it seemed, couldn't find enough things to praise.

It was her voice, of course, that got most of the compliments. Marian knew at last how it felt to read "rave notices." What the critics of Oslo and Helsinki and Copenhagen wrote about her would have made her fortune if it had appeared in the newspapers of Paris or London or Vienna. (Unfortunately, as she discovered on her return, Americans did not look to Scandinavia for authority in matters of music.)

There was only one dead spot in all the enthusiasm. That was in Stockholm. Mr. Rasmussen had turned over the management of Marian's Swedish concerts to a young and very enterprising impresario named Helmer Enwall. He was anxious to convince her that the reserve of Swedish audiences and critics was not a sign that they failed to appreciate Marian's genius.

"It is just that we Swedes are slow to make up our minds," he said. "There is a demand for a third concert here in Stockholm. My countrymen want to hear more. Sing for them again, and they will be yours. And once they are, nothing will ever change them."

Marian sang the third concert in Stockholm, and then sailed for New York.

Chapter 15

"Once in a Hundred Years"

If Marian had any hope that her Scandinavian triumphs would reecho in the American concert world, it didn't last through her first interview with the publicity department at the Judson office.

They took notes on all she told them and copied phrases from one or two of the reviews, but it was plain that they were not impressed or heartened. It was as if she had made a success in some remote corner of Siberia or Tierra del Fuego. And when requests came in for concerts on her tour, there were no new ones.

She was back in the well-worn groove. The wave of success had lifted her once again so that she could look into the golden promised land, and then let her down at the same place on the sand.

And yet, there was a difference this time. For the wave had lifted her on the other side of the ocean, not here. Here, she was in the same rut that her career had settled into after the Lewisohn Stadium concert. She had never got out of it. Unless a miracle happened she knew now that she never would.

There was not very much she could do about it, and she had a responsibility to those loyal supporters who called her back year after year. Marian started out on her tour determined to fulfill that responsibility—to give the best she had to every audience, small or large. But she was discouraged, and the irritations and hardships that resulted from American prejudice bothered her more than they had before. Now and then she found herself dreaming of that other world where she had been accepted so differently, both as a person and an artist. Absent from it, she missed that world.

And suddenly, without advance warning, there was a message from Stockholm, a cable from Director Enwall:
CAN OFFER YOU TWENTY CONCERTS.
WHEN CAN YOU COME?

It was as if he had been listening in on her daydreams. It was a great temptation. She would make no more—possibly a little less—money on 20 concerts in Scandinavia than she was making on her modest tour of 20 concerts at home. But to be truly wanted somewhere was so heart-warming. . . .
CAN OFFER FORTY CONCERTS.
CABLE REPLY.

The second offer came before she had made up her mind about the first. She talked to several people: her mother, Billy King, other friends.

"Why not divide your year in half?" someone suggested. "Sing 20 concerts here and 20 over there."

CAN OFFER YOU SIXTY CONCERTS!

The third cable did it.

Marian thought she had better answer before the figure went up to something ridiculous like a hundred. She cabled Director Enwall that she would come, but for 20 concerts only. She would have to return to the United States to fulfill her next season's schedule.

She notified the Judson office of her plans: when she would be leaving, and when she could promise to be back. They didn't seem greatly interested. She had become a matter of routine.

But in Sweden she was anything but routine.

There were more than 60 concerts lined up when she arrived. Director Enwall showed her requests from all the Scandinavian countries and Finland and Russia too; from small towns and big cities, from places she had never heard of, places where snow blanketed the ground for all but one month of the year, and the midnight sun shone round the clock during that month.

In Sweden the coolness had heated up to what one newspaperman called "a case of Marian fever." She was showered with gifts, praises, honors, and invitations. Her picture appeared in the newspapers and magazines like a movie star's picture at home.

The climax of it all, from Marian's own point of view, was an afternoon she spent in a little country home in Finland, as guest of Jean Sibelius, perhaps the greatest of then living composers. It came about like this.

[145]

Kosti had told her that it would be considered a gracious compliment if she would sing in each country at least one or two songs by their best loved composers. He helped her select and learn these additions to her regular repertory, and the results of her first experiments seemed to prove that his judgment was sound.

In Norway, she sang some of Grieg's songs and was rewarded by a note of congratulations and an invitation to visit his widow, Nina Grieg.

"For my country, you must sing something by Sibelius," Kosti said. "Perhaps we will be invited to visit him, though he is very old and sees few people. He and his wife live out in the country, not far from Helsinki."

Marian admired Sibelius's music, but she found, even with Kosti to help her, that it was difficult for her to sing. She tried one Sibelius song that had German lyrics as an encore for her Helsinki concert. The audience cheered enthusiastically, but Marian suspected that it was for her good intentions rather than her achievement.

But a day or so later Kosti called in great excitement to say they had been invited to the Villa Ainola.

"It is a great honor," he said. "We must not stay long. Half an hour, no more. You will sing two songs. We will take coffee and make our good-byes."

Marian was as delighted as Kosti—except about the prospect of singing one of his own songs for the composer. She explained to Kosti that she did not feel able to interpret them to an ordinary audience, certainly not to this extraordinary one! Kosti only shrugged it off. They would see how it turned out at the time. She must not worry about it.

[*146*]

The drive out through the wild Finnish forest country was beautiful. The Villa Ainola was small but quaintly charming; its master and mistress, utterly delightful. Sibelius was shorter than Marian had imagined him from photographs she had seen, but his head was noble, so strongly moulded that when his face was in repose he looked as if he were carved in stone.

The lady of the house made her guests comfortable with old-world courtesy. She led them into the low-ceilinged living room, drew chairs close to the bright grate fire, and then excused herself to prepare the coffee they had been invited to take.

Sibelius waved Kosti to the piano. "Now, at once!" he said heartily. "Be so good as to let me hear the voice that everyone is praising!"

Marian felt a slight pang of stage fright, but there wasn't time for more than that one pang. Kosti had already begun. It was a song she had sung many, many times in concert. She was perfectly sure of herself in it. She closed her eyes and began.

It went well.

"Another!" said her host. "Another if you please!"

Kosti struck an opening chord and raised his eyebrows in an unspoken question. It was the Sibelius song she had used as an encore. Was she willing to try it?

"Ah!" The composer knew his own work even from so small a sample. He was already leaning forward, his eyes glinting with pleasure.

Marian didn't have the heart to beg off. She nodded at Kosti and launched into the song.

"Bravo! Bravo!" Sibelius jumped to his feet as she finished, and made her a sweeping bow. "My roof is too low for your head."

(It was an old-fashioned form of compliment, but it also happened to be true. Marian felt in some danger of scraping her head as she walked under some of the lowest beams in that living room!)

Without giving her a chance to say yes or no this time, Kosti began to play another Sibelius song, one he and Marian had worked on, but which she had not tried in public. It was called "Norden," and Marian found it so haunting that she could hardly put it away, but so baffling that she knew she had not found the key to understanding it.

It eluded her even now, but she did the best she could. "Again!"

Sibelius came striding over to the piano to join them.

"That last passage before the final crescendo. Start there!" he told Kosti, and turning to Marian, "Begin a little more sadly—darkly. You understand?"

They began to work on the song together.

The half hour passed, and another was nearly gone before they knew it. With the composer himself to teach her and urge her on, Marian felt as if a veil were being lifted. What had seemed so mysterious was clear now. "Norden" was as much hers as her beloved lieder or her spirituals.

"Sing it all the way through now without interruption," said Sibelius, when he had made his last suggestion.

Marian sang.

"Champagne, not coffee," the old musician shouted to his wife. "We must celebrate!"

The six months had passed. Marian had sung more than 60 concerts, and there were still many offers that were hard to resist. Director Enwall suggested that perhaps the dates the Judson office had booked might be postponed a few weeks.

Marian cabled to ask. The answer came promptly. TEN CONCERTS CONTRACTED FOR. OTHERS UNDER CONSIDERATION. IMPOSSIBLE TO POSTPONE. ONLY ALTERNATIVE TO CANCEL.

Only ten concerts! Her American tour had shrunk to half its former size. It made no sense to go back for that. Marian cabled the Judson office to cancel.

She had cut one of the strongest ties that bound her to America—her professional one. For the first time in many years she had no concert scheduled anywhere in her homeland. There was no particular date on which she had to be back. It was an odd and not a very pleasant feeling for her.

Director Enwall took full advantage of his opportunity. Marian sang 108 concerts in the 12 months she was under his management. It was more than most people thought was good for a singer, but she wasn't tired. She sometimes felt as if she were living a fairy tale, transformed by Director Enwall's magic wand from an ordinary mortal into a musical Cinderella.

Everywhere she sang she was made to feel that she had done something deeply important for those who heard her. People told her so in every way they could: in letters; with flowers—small bunches left at her door, huge bouquets handed over the footlights at her concerts; with gifts that had once been the most precious possession of the giver. She was earning so much money that she could afford luxuries like leather bindings for her music and return gifts to her new friends. She could have sent for her mother and sisters, but she knew it was unfair to even ask them to uproot themselves and adjust their lives to herself. Besides, sooner or later she would be going back, because her roots were where theirs were.

When she thought about going back, she would remember what happened to Cinderella at the stroke of midnight. For Marian was sure her fine clothes and fairy coach would turn back into rags and a pumpkin the moment she stepped foot on a concert stage in Philadelphia or New York.

Meanwhile Director Enwall was talking of new worlds for her to conquer.

"I have a friend in Paris," he told her. "He was one of the most successful managers in Berlin until Hitler drove the Jews out of Germany. Horowitz is just beginning to build a reputation in Paris. He would be glad of a chance to present such an artist as you."

Paris was a city that had always drawn her. Perhaps it would be good to sing a concert there in the spring.

"And after that Salzburg!" Director Enwall said. "Salzburg is the music capital of the world in the summer.

You can sing your way across Europe from Paris and finish at the Festival!"

More fairy tales. But by now Marian believed anything Director Enwall prophesied might come true. She let him arrange matters with Mr. Horowitz, and set to work on an aria from a French opera for her Paris debut.

The first Paris concert went well. Mr. Horowitz was every bit as competent as Enwall had promised. The reviews were good and a second concert was announced. Marian was assured by everyone, including the Enwalls, who had come all the way from Stockholm, that she was a tremendous success.

Somehow it didn't feel quite so tremendous to her. Probably she had been spoiled by the "Marian fever" in the North. Also being this much nearer home reminded her of how very far she was from what had been her first and still was her greatest ambition.

Whatever the reason, she couldn't persuade herself that she ought to give a third concert as Mr. Horowitz advised. It was late in the season. She and Kosti had engagements to fill in Brussels and Vienna, and were due at Salzburg in July. But Mr. Horowitz was very persistent in his arguments:

A third concert would draw critics who had not come to the others. They would write even more enthusiastic reviews, because she was "catching on" with the Paris audience. These reviews would help make her way in the other cities where she was to sing for the first time.

The Enwalls had gone back to Sweden, and Marian had no one to consult but Kosti. He was for following

Mr. Horowitz's advice. Marian gave in—but against her better judgment. She was sure that Paris was empty of everyone but American tourists.

"They come to Paris to see the Folies-Bergère," she told Kosti, "but not to hear a concert by another American. I just hope this doesn't turn out to be a dreadful anticlimax."

But it was no anticlimax, thanks to a certain American tourist.

Having Sol Hurok appear unannounced in the intermission took Marian's breath away for a moment. It reminded her of the time when she had believed that if she could interest Hurok in her career, her troubles would be over. He had a reputation for managerial magic: for taking unknown artists, whom no other manager would handle, and turning them into celebrities almost overnight. Whether it was true or not, Marian believed it, but she had never been able to arrange for an audition with the magician.

Now it was too late.

She was willing to give him the chance he was asking for—to make a new career for her in America. But in her heart she didn't believe it could be done. It was seven long years since she sang with the Philharmonic at Lewisohn Stadium. As far as America was concerned, she had been going slowly downhill ever since.

If Hurok wanted to gamble, however, she would go along. She released herself from her contract with the Judson office, signed an agreement to be in New York in December for the start of a concert tour under Hurok's management. Then she put the whole thing out of her mind.

She was on her way to Vienna: city of the composers whose work meant most to her.

Schubert was born there. Beethoven and Brahms chose it as their home. It was the Holy City of music, a Mecca to all music lovers.

Marian went the rounds of places where her three composers had lived and composed and performed their works, like a pilgrim making the rounds of shrines of his patron saints: from the modest house in a quiet street that bore a sign saying Beethoven composed one of his greatest symphonies there, to the music school where young Franz Schubert earned his tuition by training choir boys for the royal chapel, to the Konzerthaus, in whose Great Hall Brahms had conducted the orchestra in first performances of his own masterworks.

Marian was to sing in the Konzerthaus, not in the Great Hall, of course, but in one of the smaller recital rooms. She didn't expect much in the way of audience or reviews. Kosti had warned her that Viennese audiences were the most difficult to please in all Europe. Almost too proud of their city's past glory, they were very slow to accept a new performer or composer.

Marian didn't care. She had other reasons for wanting to sing in Vienna, reasons that had nothing to do with advancing her career.

She was glad, though, that Kosti had warned her. Otherwise the first glimpse of her audience would have shaken her confidence. The hall was hardly half full. Marian hadn't seen such a poor crowd since that terrible night at Town Hall. (If someone had warned her then, would it have made a great difference in how she performed?)

Tonight it was easy, for she was singing to unseen listeners, the great musicians whose presence she felt everywhere in their city. Her concert was a wreath of song she was laying on their graves.

When she came to the end of the first half of the program, the applause was as much as one could hope for under the circumstances. Marian took it as a sign that she had given her best. She bowed her thanks, left the stage, rested quietly through the intermission, and came back, determined to keep the same high level to the very end.

She stared at the audience, then looked at Kosti. He was staring too.

The house was full! There were at least twice as many people as before! Where had they all come from?

Marian learned later that there was another concert going on in the Konzerthaus. The competition from it was one of the reasons for the poor attendance at hers. During the intermission, audiences from both mingled in the lobbies and corridors. What Marian's listeners had to say about her was so exciting that many people deserted the other performance to come and hear hers.

Vienna could have paid her no higher compliment.

After that came Salzburg and the Festival.

Every July for many years music lovers from all the countries of the world have been crowding into this beautiful old town in a deep valley of the Austrian Alps, to listen to a short season of opera and symphony concerts, with the world's finest conductors.

The greatest name in Salzburg that summer—and for many summers—was Arturo Toscanini.

Italian by birth, American by adoption, Maestro Toscanini was at that time conductor of the New York Philharmonic Orchestra. He had formerly conducted the orchestra at the New York Metropolitan Opera. In Salzburg he conducted both the Vienna Philharmonic and the Vienna State Opera. There was no musician living—not even Sibelius—for whom Marian felt such awe. She had come to Salzburg as much to hear him conduct as to perform herself.

Her recital was only a small affair, sponsored by a friendly singer whom Marian had first met in Philadelphia, Madame Charles Cahier. She advised her then to come to Europe to study. Delighted at how well the advice turned out, she took a personal interest in Marian and was determined to do something for her protegée. Madame Cahier hired the ballroom of one of the hotels where many of the guests and performers stayed, and sent invitations to everyone she considered important.

Marian knew that an invitation had gone to Maestro Toscanini, but she didn't think there was any possibility of his accepting it. It was well-known that he did not go to concerts while he was preparing one of his own. Even so, Marian was a little nervous. She decided not to look at her audience, not even for that moment between her bow and the time she closed her eyes to sing. It would be too easy to

*Arturo
Toscanini*

spot that famous mane of white hair and the very black brows over the intense dark eyes.

She kept her resolve and left the little stage at the end of the first half of the program without having looked once into the faces of her listeners.

Instead of the usual quiet period during intermission, there was a great bustle backstage, with many of Madame Cahier's musical friends crowding in to meet Marian and offer their congratulations. She was bowing and smiling and saying over and over, "Thank you. Thank you so very much," and envying Kosti, who was at least sitting down. Suddenly between the two people in front of her, she caught sight of the Maestro.

Her heart began to pound so that it made a roaring in her head and all but shut out the voices around her.

Marian
Anderson
Vienna,
1935

LOTTE MEITNER GRAF: HUROK ATTRACTIONS

She heard Madame Cahier presenting her, heard herself mumbling an awkward "Thank you for coming." She knew that the great man spoke to her as he bowed over her hand. But she didn't hear a single word of what he said.

"Well! That's something to put on your posters," said someone when the Maestro had gone.

"What?" Marian asked.

"Didn't you hear? 'Yours is a voice such as one hears once in a hundred years.'"

"Did he say that?" Marian turned to Madame Cahier.

"Yes, he did. Those were his very words, my dear."

A voice rang in Marian's memory. *"Your are singing like a queen and I have not yet crowned you."* One master had said that to her in London. She had understood finally

[157]

what he meant: that she had a lot to learn before she had any right to be as sure of herself as she felt that day.

Now, at last, she had been crowned. By a different Master, one whose authority was recognized everywhere in the musical world, and especially in her own beloved but inhospitable land.

She was ready now to go home.

Chapter 16

Making History

"I have never thought of myself as anything but an American," Marian said to the reporter from the Swedish news service. "My voice belongs to America. It grew here, just as I did. I could never have trained it without the help of other Americans—Negro and white—who believed in me, helped me, invested money and things even more precious than money in my career. Teachers, musicians, music lovers. Friends and people I never met.

"They gave me my start here. They made it possible for me to go abroad when that was important to me. They didn't do all this so that I could stay away. They always expected and I always intended to come home and sing."

"But if there is a prejudice that keeps you from singing here?" the reporter persisted politely. "Isn't that what's happening here in Washington?"

"I don't know," Marian said. "But this I do know. The Lord has no such prejudice. For he did give this gift to a Negro. An *American* Negro."

The hospital visit set her mind at ease about Kosti. He was certainly on the mend, already talking about how soon the doctors would let him come back to work.

"Why push yourself?" Marian asked. "The season is over. We have no more concerts. If something unexpected comes up, I can get Mr. Rupp to substitute once more."

"All right," said Kosti, with what looked like a wink in the direction of Gerald Goode. "But if you decide you need your old friend, Kosti, for moral support, remember —I'll be ready."

Goode winked back, and Marian could see that there was some delightful secret the two of them shared.

As soon as the visit was over, she asked Gerald Goode what it was.

"Let's find a quiet place here in the hospital where we can talk," he said. "I have to go back to the beginning and there'll be reporters outside."

They found a room in which expectant fathers waited to be told whether it was a boy or a girl baby. There were no fathers waiting today, and a nurse said they could sit there as long as they liked.

"I guess you know how it all began," Goode said. He went rapidly over the incidents he had incorporated into his "white paper," which had been sent to all newspapers and newspaper columnists, one of whom was Mrs. Eleanor Roosevelt.

"What Mrs. Roosevelt did gave us our first national news break," he said. After that the glare of front-page publicity was turned on everything connected with the concert and efforts to find a home for it. The foreign as well as the American press reported every new development. One of these was the application for the use of Central High School's auditorium, which was turned down by the Board of Education for the District of Columbia.

"Believe it or not, that was the first some people in this country had ever heard about Jim Crow in Washington," Goode told Marian. "They were shocked, and a lot of them wanted to do more than just say so. That's how the Marian Anderson Protest Committee came to be formed."

The first thing the Committee did was to circulate a petition addressed to the school board, asking them to reconsider their stand. When the attempt to compromise on this failed, the Protest Committee decided to call a big public meeting at which more pressure could be exerted.

"But I'm getting ahead of my own story," Goode said. "While all this was going on, you'll never guess what Hurok wanted me to do! Start looking for a park!"

"What for?—Oh!" Marian had to smile as the connection dawned on her. "A park for me to sing in?"

"That's right! Maybe you heard back in February Hurok said he'd see to it you sang in Washington within earshot of Constitution Hall, if it had to be out of doors."

"I did hear something like that, but I didn't suppose he meant it to be taken seriously."

"Neither did I at first. But one day he wanted to know what parks there were in that end of Washington, whether any of them had a bandshell, and from whom you had to ask permission to give a concert in one!" Goode shook his head at the memory of his own astonishment. "Anyway, that's what I was on my way to find out, when I ran into Walter White of the N.A.A.C.P."

Mr. White was on his way down to meet with the Protest Committee. He and Goode settled down to talk, and Goode happened to mention his problem about finding a park.

"You won't need one," White assured him. "We'll get Central High School. We may even get Constitution Hall!"

"But just in case you don't get either," Goode said, "can you think of a good park?"

"I can think of a dozen," White replied. "What sort of a park do you want?"

"A big one. Big enough for 25,000 people. Maybe more!"

"There's only one place near Constitution Hall as big as all that," said White slowly. "It's not exactly a park. I mean the Mall between Washington Monument and the Lincoln Memorial."

"The Lincoln Memorial! What a setting for a concert by Marian Anderson!"

The two men stared at each other as the idea grew and put forth leaves and flowers in their imaginations.

"Whom do we see?" asked Goode, excitedly. "The District of Columbia Park Commission? Or the Commissioner of Police?"

"Neither," said White. "That's a National Monument, so it must be under the National Park Service. That's the

Department of Interior!" He snapped his fingers and his eyes lighted up. "I know someone there. I'll put in a call from the station and see if we can make an appointment to go in and talk to him."

Walter White came back from the phone booth in the station to say they were to take a taxi and go straight to the offices of the Department of Interior.

When they left there, an hour or so later, they had an assurance that the Secretary of the Interior would consider a free concert by Marian Anderson to be "a good use of the public facilities"—provided a recognized organization sponsored the event.

"That was when I first got the notion about quitting my job," Goode told Marian.

"What do you mean? Have you quit your job with Mr. Hurok?" she asked in distress.

"Not yet. But I'm going to, on the day the Marian Anderson Concert Committee is formed."

"Concert Committee? I thought you said it was a Protest Committee."

"I don't blame you for getting confused," Goode said, smiling. "Things change so fast around here, I can't follow myself. Let me go back to the point where White and I talked to Oscar Chapman at the Department of Interior."

They learned from him that Secretary Harold L. Ickes had already sent a protest to the D.A.R. But Chapman, who was Assistant Secretary, was so angry that he wanted to go farther. He had heard there was to be a public meeting, and he offered himself as chairman.

"That's the meeting I told you about this morning. It's called by the Marian Anderson Protest Committee, at the big Metropolitan African Methodist Church here in Washington this Sunday," Goode explained. "It's a last-ditch attempt to persuade the Board of Education to give us Central High School with no strings attached." He paused for her reaction.

"Do you think it can succeed?" Marian asked.

"I—don't know," Goode said, doubtfully.

"If it doesn't, what then?"

"Then Mordecai Johnson, who is president of Howard University and honorary chairman of the Concert Series, will make formal application to the Secretary of the Interior for the use of Lincoln Memorial and the lawn in front of it for a free public concert on Easter Sunday. If that permission is granted—and it will be—there'll be a Marian Anderson Concert Committee that can use my services, full time."

Marian raised her eyes to look into his.

"Can you explain to me why this is so important to you?" she asked.

"To me personally?"

"Yes. Because it isn't a personal concern. It can't be. We've known each other professionally for a couple of years, and it's been a pleasant relationship. But we've never had an opportunity to become friends. You have no other particular interest, it seems to me. You're not a musician, or a public servant of any kind, or a minister. . . . What is it that makes you talk about quitting your job to work on a free concert?"

[164]

"It *is* a personal concern," Goode said quietly. "For many reasons. One is that I'm a Jew. What's happening in Germany today began when Hitler denied Jewish artists and doctors and teachers the right to practice their professions. Next he took their jobs away from Jewish working-men, their shops away from Jewish tradesmen, and their businesses away from Jewish businessmen. Then their homes and their savings. Then their liberty.

"Thousands have had to leave the country—their own country, where they were born and their fathers were born. Those who didn't leave in time will be killed. It has begun already.

"That's one reason I have a very personal concern about prejudice.

"Besides," he added more lightly, "it isn't every day a man has a chance to put everything he knows about his job to work on something much bigger than a job. This concert is going to make history."

Chapter 17

"Genius Draws No Color Line"

The big church was SRO, as they say in show business, meaning that there was standing room only.

On the platform where the pulpit stood, were the speakers and sponsors of the Protest Meeting: Oscar Chapman, Assistant Secretary of the Interior; Mary McLeod Bethune, venerable Director of Negro Affairs for the National Youth Administration; a white professor of Christian ethics from the Virginia Theological Seminary; the Negro president of Howard University; Congresswoman Caroline O'Day of New York, who was originally from Georgia; Charles Houston, Negro attorney who represented Howard University in the school board hearings.

There were others who had wanted to be there and sent telegrams of greeting, which were read aloud from the platform. One was from a famous Senator—whose bills had established the rights of labor in the New Deal.

THE MARIAN ANDERSON CASE IS NOT A
LOCAL ISSUE. IT IS A MATTER OF FORE-
MOST NATIONAL AND INTERNATIONAL IM-
PORTANCE. IF ART CAN BE STIFLED AND
RACIAL LINES DRAWN SO TIGHTLY IN
OUR CAPITAL CITY, THEN IT WOULD BE
WELL FOR US TO PONDER THE FATE OF
DEMOCRACY IN THE U.S.

ROBERT WAGNER

Senator Wagner's telegram made headlines all over
the country. But the dramatic climax of the evening was
the speech by Charles Houston.

He spoke of the excuses given for the refusal of both
Constitution Hall and Central High School: that segregation was traditional in Washington and therefore sacred;
that white people wanted and had a right to protection
against contact with their fellow citizens of different color.

"The tradition of white artists only in Constitution
Hall is not old enough to be sacred," he said somewhat
sarcastically. "It was written into the bylaws less than seven
years ago!"

Whether or not Washington concertgoers wanted to
be "protected" by Jim Crow rulings he could not say. "But
the students at Central High School are not grateful for
this sort of protection. I know it, and I can prove it to you."

He held up a paper—a proof copy of Leon Smith's
editorial for the Central High *Bulletin*.

"Here is one expression of student opinion. None of
you have read it, because it was not printed. It was sup-
pressed! Would you like to hear it now?"

[*168*]

"Yes! Read it!" the audience roared.

Houston read the whole of the short editorial, down to its concluding sentence, which said:

Let us hope that it [the Board] does reconsider [its decision] and do Central the honor of playing host to one of the musical world's greatest artists, as well as prove to the rest of the world that this country holds no grudges because of race or color.

As soon as Mr. Houston had finished speaking, Congressman Joseph Gavagan of New York rose to say that he intended to offer a resolution in Congress for an investigation of the suppression of the editorial and other expressions of student opinion. Congressman James McGranery of Pennsylvania, who was also on the platform, announced he would support the resolution.

Resolutions were drawn up and submitted to the meeting. They were passed with thunderous voice votes. One went to the President General of the D.A.R. One went to the Principal of Central High School. The most important one, of course, went to the Board of Education.

That was Sunday night.

The next day—March 27, 1939—passed without any reply from the Board of Education.

The next day—Tuesday—Marian was at home, in the quiet little house on South Martin Street in Philadelphia, across from the Union Baptist Church.

[*169*]

The phone rang. She answered. It was New York. Sol Hurok calling.

"Guess what?" he said cheerfully. "We have a request for you to sing in Washington."

Marian's heart seemed to stop.

"Where?" she asked cautiously.

"At the White House. The King and Queen of England are coming to visit. Mrs. Roosevelt and the President want you to sing for their guests."

(*"Did you sing for the King and Queen?" the Judson Office publicity man had asked her once, and she had said no, of course not!*)

"Shall we accept?" Hurok asked.

"Yes, of course."

"Good. Now—we have another request. You remember there was a date on your schedule for April 9."

Marian's heart seemed to stop a second time.

"In Washington?"

"Right. Would you be willing to sing under different auspices?," Hurok asked, as if this were a routine request. "A free public concert, on the steps of the Lincoln Memorial?"

"Must I?"

The words burst out without her intending them to.

"You don't want to?" Hurok sounded shocked.

"It's not a question of what I want," she said. (The very thought of singing under such circumstances, as the center of so bitter a controversy, to a crowd of the size Goode had estimated went against the grain of her character and her feeling about singing. But she had thought

[*170*]

about it enough to have reached one decision at least: that her personal feelings were of little importance at this moment.) "What I'm wondering," she said aloud, "is whether I *ought* to."

"Why not?"

"Will it help? Or make things worse?"

"Listen, Marian," Hurok said seriously. "You don't think it's right to have a ban against Negro performers in Constitution Hall?"

"No. Nor in any public place. Nor against the members of any group. But I'm not sure this is the way to go about removing the ban. The change has to be made in people's hearts. Will giving this concert make that change come sooner? Or postpone it even longer?"

"Nobody can say for sure," Hurok admitted. "I for one don't pretend to understand what goes on in the hearts —or the heads!—of people who don't want you to sing any place. But I tell you there are 100,000 people whose hearts will be heavy if you do not sing on Easter Sunday, because they are planning to come and listen to you!"

"One hundred thousand? You're exaggerating!"

"More than that! There will be radio hookups from here to the Pacific. Counting those who will listen but not see, there will be millions. Maybe it is about them you should be thinking when you give your answer!"

"All right," Marian said. "I'll do as well as I can."

Easter Sunday dawned cloudy and cold.

At the Lincoln Memorial a temporary stage had been set up on the wide terrace from which steps led up toward the marble colonnade and down to the lawn and the reflecting pool. On this level space rows of chairs had been placed for sponsors of the concert and distinguished guests. In the center was the piano and a little in front of it a rostrum for the speakers and the singer. There were six microphones to carry the speeches and the music out over the great expanse of the Mall, and over the much greater expanse of America on radio waves.

On all the approaches to the area there were barricades to halt automobile traffic, and roped-off aisles to channel the flow of foot traffic that was expected. There were hundreds of extra Park Service and regular city police.

Everything was set. Everything but the weather.

Anything was possible in Washington in early April.

It might rain. It might snow. It might stay cloudy and cold. It might turn gloriously sunny and warm. It made a great deal of difference which of these things it was doing by noon, when many thousands would be making up their minds whether to come out or stay home and listen on the radio. There were many people who would come in any case—unless there was a downpour so heavy that the affair had to be cancelled. But there were many who couldn't take a chance on getting drenched in a sudden shower, or chilled by standing for two hours in a raw wind. Old people, very young people, or people with very young children and no one to leave them with. These might have to settle for hearing, but not seeing or being seen.

If that happened to many of the thousands expected, something would be lost. Lost to each individual, whether he came or stayed home, and lost to the watching world:

[172]

the image of Americans gathered in great numbers to pay homage to a great Negro American artist. An affirmation of the strength of an American idea that was in conflict with an American prejudice!

Many people prayed in their churches that morning in Washington that the sun would be shining by the time services were over.

Marian came down on an early train so that she would have plenty of time.

She and Kosti were driven to the Memorial to try out the piano and the microphones. Policemen were already closing the roads to automobiles. A few people were already wandering like lost sheep along the pool in which the thin white spar of the Washington Monument was darkly reflected. They were so few that they made the Mall look bigger and emptier than usual.

It would, Kosti guessed soberly, take no less than 50,000 people to make a respectable showing. Was such an audience possible on such a day?

When the short rehearsal was over, Marian was driven to the home of the Gifford Pinchots. Mr. Pinchot had once been governor of Marian's home state and was still active in national politics. He and Mrs. Pinchot received Marian as an honored guest, and gave her a quiet room in which she could change into her concert gown and rest.

It seemed a very short time before there was a knock on her door. It was time to go to the Memorial.

There was a police escort for her car now, with sirens to clear a path through the snarl of traffic near the Mall.

[173]

The car stopped as close to the Memorial as it could get, at a sidewalk that led to the back entrance. Marian made her way between lines of tightly packed spectators, all obviously friendly. On one side of her walked Sol Hurok; on the other side, her old friend and attorney, Hubert Delany, Commissioner of Internal Revenue in New York, one of the few Negroes to hold high public office at that time.

As the three of them approached the entrance, Oscar Chapman stepped forward to greet them. At exactly the same instant, the sun came out like a torch.

No stage manager could have arranged such an effect. Everyone watching cheered.

Marian was waiting in the sanctuary where the great Daniel French statue of Lincoln stands. Carved into the marble on one wall she read the words of his great Second Inaugural Address:

WITH MALICE TOWARD NONE, WITH CHARITY FOR ALL, WITH FIRMNESS IN THE RIGHT AS GOD GIVES US TO SEE THE RIGHT, LET US STRIVE ON TO FINISH THE WORK WE ARE IN . . .

On the opposite wall was Lincoln's immortal definition of the United States:

. . . A NEW NATION, CONCEIVED IN LIBERTY AND DEDICATED TO THE PROPOSITION THAT ALL MEN ARE CREATED EQUAL.

He had spoken those words on a battlefield of a war to test that proposition. The crowd at which the gigantic seated figure seem to gaze was here today to take part in another such test.

Marian could hear the strange, faraway roaring of that crowd, something like what one hears from a great conch shell held close to the ear. She tried not to wonder how large or how small the crowd was, or how it compared to what had been wanted. But those on stage could see the crowd, and the crowd could see them: a most impressive array of dignitaries in their formal Sunday best, the men in tall black hats and overcoats, the ladies muffled in furs.

The list of names on the program was even more impressive; for it included sponsors who, like Mrs. Roosevelt, were there in spirit, but physically unable to attend. "A Who's Who in Washington," someone said: from the Chief Justice of the Supreme Court to the heads of the two great labor federations; members of the President's cabinet and leaders of the opposition party; senators and congressmen; Negroes and whites; Republican and Democrats; Northerners and Southerners. There was the name of a famous stage actress whose father was a senator from Alabama (and almost surely a supporter of rigid segregation). There was the name of a Supreme Court Justice who was known to have once been a member of the Ku Klux Klan. There was the name of the Mayor of New York; a Washington newspaper publisher; a Polish-born symphony conductor; a Catholic monsignor; an Episcopal canon; an American operatic soprano.

Newspaper men were not only taking notes on these and other celebrities who were there or listed as sponsors; they were also noting who was not there and not listed. There would be some who would regret tomorrow that they had not been seen here today, some whose political ambitions would suffer for their lack of interest or courage.

Now one man whose courage no one ever questioned rose and walked to the microphones. Square-shouldered, square-jawed Harold Ickes, Secretary of the Interior, famous "curmudgeon" of the New Deal. It was his duty as host to welcome the crowd and guests, and to introduce the artist. He was known as a forceful and effective speaker, but no one had ever heard him speak as he did now:

> In this great auditorium under the sky all of us are free. When God gave us this wonderful outdoors and the sun, the moon and the stars, He made no distinction of race or creed or color. And 130 years ago He sent to us one of His truly great in order that he might restore freedom to those from whom we had disregardfully taken it. In carrying out this task, Abraham Lincoln laid down his life, and so it is as appropriate as it is fortunate that today we stand reverently and humbly at the base of this memorial to the great emancipator while glorious tribute is rendered his memory by a daughter of the race from which he struck the chains of slavery.
>
> Facing us down the Mall beyond the Washington Monument, which we have erected as a symbol of the towering stature and fame of him who founded this Republic, there is rising a memorial to that other great democrat in our short history, Thomas Jefferson, who proclaimed that principle of equality of opportunity which Abraham Lincoln

believed in so implicitly and took so seriously. In our own time, too many pay mere lip service to these twin planets in our democratic heaven. There are some, even in this great Capital of our democratic Republic, who are either too timid or too indifferent to lift up the light that Jefferson and Lincoln carried aloft.

Genius, like justice, is blind. For genius has touched with the tip of her wing this woman who, if it had not been for the great mind of Lincoln, would not be able to stand among us today a free individual in a free land. Genius draws no color line. She has endowed Marian Anderson with such a voice as lifts any individual above his fellows, as is a matter of exultant pride to any race. And so it is fitting that Marian Anderson should raise her voice in tribute to the noble Lincoln, whom mankind will ever honor.

We are grateful to Miss Marian Anderson for coming here to sing for us today.

While the crowd was still cheering the introduction, two figures appeared from the colonnade and started down the wide steps: a white man and a dark woman. She was very tall, and she wore a brown fur coat below which a green and gold brocade dress fanned out like a train.

Everyone could see her stop and look out at the crowd. Did she sway slightly? It was hard to tell.) She bowed her head, as if in acknowledgement of the applause, and continued down the stairs. Calm and queenly she stood at the rostrum, behind the microphones . . . waiting for quiet.

[177]

What Marian saw as she looked at was a sea of faces. She had never understood what that worn-out expression meant till now. It was a solid, gently moving surface in which faces—all shapes and shades of brown and white—were blurred together, dotted with thousands and thousands of eyes, all staring at her.

There were more than the 50,000 people Kosti had said it would take to make the Mall "respectably full." There might be 75,000—even 100,000. A crowd this size was too big for her to estimate.

Much too big! It was overwhelming.

She had always believed that excitement was good for a singer. It sent blood coursing quicker and harder through veins and arteries, stimulating the body to put forth that extra spurt of energy that was needed for a fine performance. But this excitement went beyond that.

Her throat seemed to be closing, choking off the sound before it was born. Her pulse was pounding so hard in her temples that she could hear nothing else. It was like the time in Salzburg when she saw Toscanini coming toward her. It was worse. . . .

Kosti must have struck the opening chords of "America." She guessed because she knew it was to be played first, and she saw—rather than heard—quiet come over the sea out there.

She wished desperately that she were standing in the sheltering curve of the piano. Then she could have *felt* the music of the accompaniment. But it was out of the question. She had to be here, close to the microphones.

They were waiting for her now.

[*178*]

Lincoln Memorial Concert, Easter, 1939

For one terrible moment she could not think of the first words of the anthem she knew as well as her name!

(". . . *there is still the audience. The piano begins. They are waiting for you to make the first note . . . That is when you call on what you know!*")

Marian could hear Mr. Boghetti's voice in the studio, years ago. She knew that he was here today. She could imagine his eye fixed on her, commanding her, hypnotizing her into being the professional he had taught her to be.

She forced herself to breathe naturally, regularly, not too fast, not too deep. She called on everything she had learned, not only from her teachers, but from her own experience. The how and the why!

It worked.

Her pulse pounded not quite so hard. Her throat relaxed. The words came into her mind.

She nodded to Kosti. She heard the chords as he struck them this time.

> *My country, tis of thee,*
> *Sweet land of liberty,*
> *Of thee I sing. . . .*

All across the sweet land people listened.

In California, college students who had taken portable radios and picnic baskets listened from the hillsides overlooking San Francisco Bay. In Georgia, other students listened in the chapel of the college where Marian had sung on her first long trip away from home. In Seattle, a grandmother taking care of her nine-year-old grandson while his mother was busy with a new baby, listened. In Washington, D.C., the grandfather of the same little boy and the new baby, sat in his wheel chair, in a big house on Pennsylvania Avenue, listening. . . .

> *Land where our fathers died,*
> *Land of the Pilgrims' pride. . .*

In towns in Texas and towns in New England, sons and daughters of the first Pilgrims, and of many, many pilgrims who had come since, listened.

> *From every mountain side,*
> *Let freedom ring!*

It was not a long concert.

Marian sang the aria she had sung to win the Lewissohn Stadium contest. She sang Schubert's lovely "Ave Maria." She sang three spirituals, one of them her favorite, which always brought into her mind an image of her people, struggling patiently, persistently, with reverent faith, against odds.

Trampin', trampin',
Tryin' to make Heaven my home.
I've never been to Heaven,
But I've been told
That the streets up there
Are paved with gold.
Tryin' to make Heaven my home. . . .

Those who heard her that day saw in their mind's eye the same sort of image, and foresaw the end of her people's long pilgrimage. For Marian Anderson had indeed become a symbol of something greater than herself.

"A symbol of the willing acceptance of the immortal truth that all men are created free and equal."

Epilogue

The concert at Lincoln Memorial was not the end, but a new beginning for Marian Anderson.

Another great wave had lifted her and carried her farther than she had looked even in dreams.

Professionally, there were no more worlds to conquer. She was at the top. Her fee—already as high as that of any concert singer—doubled after the Easter Sunday concert. Within a year or two, she was earning about a third of a million dollars a year from concerts, recordings, radio and later television appearances.

There were no bars to performances by her, even in Constitution Hall. Hardly a year after the rejection that boomeranged, she was invited to sing there in a concert to raise funds for a war charity. For the war that had been threatening since Hitler and his Brown Shirts took over in Germany, finally broke out. (If Marian had gone to Berlin a year later, she could not have sung in the Bachsaal, for by that time only "Aryans" were welcome.)

As the Nazi armies swept across Europe, and America joined in the fight against them, many old walls of prejudice crumbled here. What people accepted at first as a war-time measure, began to seem more normal than what had gone before. So when Marian sang two charity concerts in Constitution Hall, and then in January, 1943, one on her own, it caused no particular excitement in any quarter.

As for Marian, she had no feeling of triumph or of bitterness about this victory. By then she was involved in meeting much more rewarding challenges, such as, for instance, her first operatic role.

When she appeared as Ulrica, the sorceress, in Verdi's *The Masked Ball*, no Negro had ever sung with the New York Metropolitan. (Another of Mr. Boghetti's prophecies had finally come true.) Although she preferred to go on with concert work instead of shifting to a new musical form, her appearance was so successful that it opened the way for other Negro singers to become great stars of America's opera stage.

She married and founded a second home of her own (She would never be able to think of herself as having left the home on South Martin Street, where her mother and her sisters and nephew still lived.)

Honors continued to be awarded her. A medal for the most distinguished achievement by an American Negro. A prize in the name of a famous Philadelphia philanthropist for the person who had done most to bring honor

At the Marian Anderson Playground, 1954

to that city. A medal from the King of Sweden. The key to more than one American city.

One honor which meant a great deal to her, but which she could neither wear around her neck nor put in the bank, was the naming of a recreation center built by government funds in her own South Philadelphia neighborhood. In this fine building and playground, children of all colors who grow up as she did can enjoy advantages she did not: the best of facilities for healthy and creative play —for learning art and music and drama and crafts, for playing games and sports, including the one Marian never did learn. There is a fine swimming pool on the grounds of the Marian Anderson Center.

But perhaps the most important of all—the climax of her public life as an artist and an American—came nearly twenty years after the Easter Sunday on which she was at last accepted as a first-class citizen of her own country.

In 1957 the United States sent Marian Anderson on an official embassy of goodwill to the other side of the world. She sang her way across Asia—met everywhere by huge crowds of admirers, many thousands of them children.

They sang to her and she sang to them. Sometimes the music was so different that it was to be wondered that the message of each side was clear to the other. But music is as close to a universal language as man has yet made for himself.

America's First Lady of Song spoke for all of America to all the world not only in music but in her very person, the facts of her life. She had become a symbol of yet another sort—the capacity to dream big and to work hard to make the big dreams come true, a quality which is the best of America.

*Marian
Anderson
fans on the
State Depart-
ment tour*

Harold Ickes and Marian Anderson, 1939

*First act curtain call, the Met, with
Roberta Peters and Leonard Warren*

*Sorting music
at home, 1954*

At the United Nations General Assembly, with (left to right) James J. Wadsworth, John Foster Dulles, George McGregor, 1958

Mrs. Roosevelt and Marian Anderson, 1958

Curtain call, Taiwan Normal University, 1957

[189]

ACKNOWLEDGEMENTS

For help in researching the facts of this story, I should like to thank Dorothy and James Bolle, Virginia Erdesz, Gerald Goode, Sol Hurok and Michael Sweeley, Eugenia Langford, Librarian, and Ralph Russell of the Department of Interior, and Dorothy Porter, Librarian of the Moorland Foundation, Howard University.

April 1, 1963   Janet Stevenson